Luc Besson

MANCHESTER
UNIVERSITY PRESS

FRENCH FILM DIRECTORS

DIANA HOLMES and ROBERT INGRAM *series editors*

forthcoming titles

FRENCH FILM DIRECTORS

Luc Besson

SUSAN HAYWARD

Manchester University Press
MANCHESTER AND NEW YORK

distributed exclusively in the USA by St. Martin's Press

Published by Manchester University Press
Oxford Road, Manchester M13 9NR, UK
and Room 400, 175 Fifth Avenue, New York, NY 10010, USA

Distributed exclusively in the USA by
St. Martin's Press, Inc., 175 Fifth Avenue, New York,
NY 10010, USA

Distributed exclusively in Canada by
UBC Press, University of British Columbia, 6344 Memorial Road,
Vancouver, BC, Canada V6S 1Z2

British Library Cataloguing-in-Publication Data
A catalogue record is available from the British Library

Library of Congress Cataloging-in-Publication Data applied for

ISBN 0 7190 5075 8 *hardback*
   0 7190 5076 6 *paperback*

First published 1998

01 00 99 98   10 9 8 7 6 5 4 3 2 1

Typeset in Scala with Meta display
by Koinonia Limited, Manchester
Printed in Great Britain
by Biddles Ltd, Guildford and King's Lynn

For Jae
and with thanks

Contents

List of plates

All stills courtesy of BFI Stills, Posters and Designs

Series editors' foreword

To an anglophone audience, the combination of the words 'French' and 'cinema' evokes a particular kind of film: elegant and wordy, sexy but serious – an image as dependent upon national stereotypes as is that of the crudely commercial Hollywood blockbuster, which is not to say that either image is without foundation. Over the past two decades, this generalised sense of a significant relationship between French identity and film has been explored in scholarly books and articles, and has entered the curriculum at university level and, in Britain, at A-level. The study of film as art-form and (to a lesser extent) as industry has become a popular and widespread element of French Studies, and French cinema has acquired an important place within Film Studies. Meanwhile, the growth in multi-screen and 'art-house' cinemas, together with the development of the video industry, has led to the greater availability of foreign-language films to an English-speaking audience. Responding to these developments, this series is designed for students and teachers seeking information and accessible but rigorous critical study of French cinema, and for the enthusiastic filmgoer who wants to know more.

The adoption of a director-based approach raises questions about *auteurism*. A series that categorises films not according to period or to genre (for example), but to the person who directed them, runs the risk of espousing a romantic view of film as the product of solitary inspiration, On this model, the critic's role might seem to be that of discovering continuities, revealing a necessarily coherent set of themes and motifs which correspond to the particular genius of the individual. This is not our aim: the *auteur* perspective on film, itself most clearly articulated in France in the early 1950s, will be interrogated in certain volumes of the series, and throughout the director will be treated as one highly significant element in a complex process of film production and reception which includes socio-economic and political determinants, the work of a large and highly skilled team of artists and technicians, the mechanisms of production and distribution, and the complex and multiply determined responses of spectators.

The work of some of the directors in the series is already well known outside France, that of others is less so – the aim is both to provide informative and original English-language studies of established figures, and to extend the range of French Directors known to anglophone students of cinema. We intend the series to contribute to the promotion of the formal and informal study of French films, and to the pleasure of those who watch them.

DIANA HOLMES
ROBERT INGRAM

Luc Besson
the emerging filmmaker

Introduction

> Confronter son intellectualisme à une pensée populaire est un
> acte généreux. Exhiber son intellectualisme, sans retour, est un
> acte orgueilleux et nombriliste, qui va à l'encontre même de l'art!
>   L'art se doit d'être généreux et populaire et si l'art ne rend pas
> meilleur, alors l'art ne sert à rien.[1]

This quotation from Luc Besson's book of the film *Léon* aptly
sums up this director's entire conflictual relationship with the so-
called heavyweights of French film criticism (*Positif, Cahiers du
Cinéma*) and to a certain degree with the French film industry
itself. And just as his own book or, indeed, series of books on his
films seek to demystify production practices and are designed to
act as guides to filmmaking, so too this present volume on his
work is intended to provide readings of the 'popular' of his work as
it meets up with the intellectualism of which he speaks.

Besson's work, with the exception of his first feature film (*Le
Dernier Combat*, 1983) which was liked by almost all those
engaged in film criticism, has been acclaimed by the popular film
journals (such as *Première*) and excoriated by the more serious
ones (such as *Cahiers du Cinéma* and *Positif*). However, all of his

---

1 Besson, Luc (1995) *L'Histoire de Léon*, Paris, Intervista, 170. 'To cross-fertilise
one's intellectualism with popular thought is a generous thing to do. To exhibit
one's intellectualism, without any give or take is a navel-gazing act of pride
which contradicts the whole purpose of art. Art should be expansive and popular
and if it cannot be then it serves no purpose.'

films (seven in all to date[2]) have been huge successes with the main audience of the 1980s and 1990s – the so-called youth class of 15 to 35 years of age. Besson makes no claim to being an *auteur* and refers to himself as *metteur en scène*. Indeed, he says he makes neither art nor culture, rather he tells stories. And the stories he tells are of individuals who experience great difficulty in adapting to society, who are prevented from achieving their goals because they are in a state of 'dis-ease' with society – a society, Besson claims, that has seriously 'unbalanced the family, creating emotional deprivation in young people up to the age of 20'.[3] His films are, he states, his way of fighting against this. Given the huge appeal of his work (his audiences are in the millions), it is clear that Besson is a filmmaker who makes films that are perceived as signs of their time. And this is one reason at least why his films merit serious investigation.

If Besson has not endeared himself to film critics it is in part due to his resistance to what he perceives as their hypocrisy – something he first encountered in relation to his very first feature film *Le Dernier Combat* which he submitted to the 1983 Avoriaz Science Fiction Film Festival. As he records it, not one critic or film journal was interested in interviewing him about the film.[4] But once it had swept the major awards at the Festival (the Critics and the Special Jury Prizes), then he was hotly in demand. He was even saluted as the new Stephen Spielberg who had won the same prizes at the 1972 Avoriaz Festival.[5] The only exception to this comportment was Michèle Halberstadt who at that time worked for Radio 7. She invited Besson and his team for an interview prior to the announcement of the prizes. Since that time, she has become the editor of *Première* – the only film journal Besson seems to interview with in France. Besson has also infuriated critics because, ever since the panning he received for *Le Grand Bleu* (1988), he has refused to première his films, preferring to

---

2 At the time of going to press, Besson's latest film *Le Cinquième Elément* has just been released. A brief review of this latest film appears in the Postscript.

3 Besson quoted in *The Observer Review*, 30.10.94.

4 Besson (1993) *L'Histoire du Dernier Combat*, Paris, Bordas et fils, 150.

5 For more details see Besson (1993) 150–154.

give them general release to 'his' audiences who were responsible for saving this film from being consigned to oblivion.

Nor has he particularly endeared himself to the French film industry which he finds lazy and stultifying. This is how he describes it when he was trying to get production money for his first film in the early 1980s:

> Au début des années 1980, on produisait beaucoup, c'était la bonne époque du cinéma. La société Artmedia dominait tout ça. Elle montait des *packages*, c'est-à-dire qu'elle prenait ses propres auteurs, ses propres acteurs, ses propres metteurs en scène et qu'elle sortait de bons petits films qui allaient nourrir les multisalles...
>
> Si bien qu'en dix ans, le parc cinématographique français s'est appauvri, la fréquentation des salles a chuté de 50%, car plus on fait de films 'moyens', moins les gens ont envie d'aller au cinéma. Et le plus terrible, c'est que lorsque les gens perdent l'habitude d'y aller, ils prennent l'habitude de s'occuper autrement, ce qui est mortel pour le cinéma.[6]

All filmmakers encounter difficulty obtaining funds, and Besson is no exception. But what he is pointing to here are the problems that occur when the industry becomes monopolistic or moves into a cartel mentality and plays safe. There is very little space for innovation and renovation of the cinema, or ultimately of giving the audiences variety. Besson's enormous success, particularly since the great popularity of *Le Grand Bleu*, has meant he has had considerable freedom to dictate his terms and make the films he wants the way he wants.[7]

6 Besson (1993) 30. 'At the beginning of the 1980s the industry was producing a lot, it was the good years in cinema. The Artmedia Production Company dominated the whole show. It created package-deals, that is, it used its own writers, actors, directors and made nice little films to supply the multi-screen cinema complexes ... The effect in ten years was that the French film marketplace had become greatly impoverished. Audience attendance fell by 50 per cent, because the more you make average films, the less people feel like going to see them. And the worst thing is that when people lose the habit of going to the cinema, they find other things to occupy their free time, and that's death for the cinema.'

7 Besson is not particularly enamoured of the French government's policy on funding films either since it discriminates against films which are ostensibly

Before entering further into these various issues, however, it is important to give a contextual framework to this enormously popular filmmaker. The purpose of this introductory chapter is to situate Besson, first, in relation to his formative years based purely on interviews and the biographical details he has released (Besson is very private about his personal life), including his early years on the film scene working across all the jobs from 'go-for/gofer', to casting, from film assistant to editing assistant; and, second, in relation to his own thinking and practices in the domain of cinema technology and the texts he produces. What emerges from this contextualising is a profile of the filmmaker Besson: his convictions, his anti-establishmentarianism, how he is both a renovator and a filmmaker continuing earlier traditions of French cinema prevalent, first, in the 1930s (particularly the practice of team work) and, later, in the Nouvelle Vague period of the late 1950s (being producer-director and technology-conscious).

Besson's formative years: 'il y a du dauphin dans tout ça'

Besson was born in Paris on 18 March 1959. His birth sign then is Pisces, the fish. And the sea, even more particularly the dolphin, has always been his first love. In the only official mini-autobiography he states clearly: 'je ne suis pas un enfant des villes. Je suis un enfant de la mer, des rochers brûlants'.[8] Although born in Paris, he spent the greater part of his childhood on the islands of Greece and (former) Yugoslavia where, during the summer months, both his mother and father worked as scuba-diving instructors for the Club Méditerrannée. In those early years, Besson's ambition, fired by a first marking encounter with a dolphin at the age of 10, was to become a *delphinologue* (a specialist

---

'French' but shot in English (as was the case for Besson's *Le Grand Bleu* and *Léon*). Conversely the government is quite happy to finance films shot in French and pay for them to be dubbed into English. Apparently the logic runs that the criterion for the nationality of a film is which language it is shot in!

8 Besson (1993) 12, 'I am not a child of the cities. I am a child of the sea and burning rocks'.

on dolphins) and to discover whether human beings could speak with dolphins. The way in which Besson describes this encounter is worth detailing here because it provides clues to the determination with which he pursued his major film project *Le Grand Bleu*, to say nothing of the drive and persistence which allowed him to become a filmmaker in the first instance. One afternoon, whilst at sea, he and the boat's captain noticed a dolphin's fin in the distance, they approached it and the 10-year-old Besson slipped into the water. Besson continues with the story thus:

> Je me mets à l'eau et, au bout de quelques minutes, il est collé à moi et me donne son aileron pour me promener. Il m'offre son ventre pour le caresser. Il me parle, il m'écoute, il me sourit. Au bout de trois heures, je me suis aperçu que le petit bruit qui gênait mon oreille, c'était le capitaine qui hurlait sous la lune pour que je remonte sur le bateau ...
>
> Je venais de rencontrer un être qui vit dans l'eau ... un être qui, sans même vous connaître, est prêt à jouer, à s'offrir à vous, à vous donner du temps et de l'amour sans compter ...
>
> Je ne venais pas de rencontrer un animal, mais un modèle de vie. Une de celles qu'on choisirait, si on n'en avait qu'une ... Le dauphin ne fait que trois choses dans la journée: il mange, il joue, il fait l'amour.
>
> Il ne connaît pas l'agression, il n'a même pas la notion de ce que cela veut dire ...
>
> Des histoires comme celle-ci, j'en ai vécues des dizaines depuis. Elles m'ont toutes bouleversé. Bien plus que celles des humains, qui ne parlent que d'honneur, de propriété, de vengeance et d'amour égoïste. Rien de tout cela ne m'intéresse.[9]

9 Besson quoted in *Première*, no. 134, May 1988, 88. 'I jumped into the water and after a few minutes he stuck to me and offered me his fin to take me for a ride. He offered me his stomach so that I could caress it. He spoke to me, listened to me, smiled at me. After three hours I realised that the tiny noise I could hear in my ear was the captain yelling to me in the moonlight to come on up ... I had just encountered a living being who lived in the water ... a being who without even knowing you is prepared to play, to give himself up to you, to give you time and love without counting ... I had encountered not just an animal but a model for life. A model one would choose if one only had the choice ... The dolphin does only three things all day: he eats, plays, makes love. He knows no aggression, he does not even know what that means ... I have experienced many more encounters like this one. They have all had a tremendous impact on me. Far

The next major sea adventure or encounter Besson mentions as strongly affecting his life was a short documentary he saw at the age of 16 on the free-diving champion Jacques Mayol. The footage showed Mayol plummeting down 92 metres unassisted by oxygen cylinders and holding his breath for four minutes. By now, Besson was himself an accomplished scuba-diver instructor but he was dumbfounded by such a feat and most particularly by the look on Mayol's face which he described as follows:

> Ce n'est pas le fait de le voir descendre dans le noir, sans respirer pendant quatre minutes, et subir des pressions énormes qui me faisait pleurer, c'est de me rendre compte que, dans ce qui me paraissait un cauchemar, lui se sentait bien! Il avait la banane, le sourire, il était décontracté!
>
> J'étais médusé. Quelle porte avait-il ouverte dans sa tête pour trouver du bonheur dans un tel cauchemar? Que voyait-il dans ce noir insondable? Je ne sais pas ce qu'il voyait, mais il le voyait, et ça le rendait terriblement heureux ...'[10]

From that moment he had, as he puts it, 'le bleu dans la tête' (literally, the sea on his brain). However, one year later, a diving accident that seriously affected his sinuses put paid to all his dreams of becoming a *delphinologue*. He was told he would never dive again. Remarkably and courageously, by the time he came to make *Le Grand Bleu*, he had determined that he would shoot the underwater scenes – so proving the experts wrong.

However, this was 1976, Besson was 17, still at school and his future dreams shattered: 'j'ai quitté mon doux rêve ouaté brutalement'.[11] As Besson himself explains, this traumatic event

---

more so than encounters with human beings who speak only of honour, property, vengeance and selfish love. None of that is of any interest to me.'

10 *Ibid.*, 90. 'It was not the fact of seeing him descending into the black water without breathing for four minutes, and experiencing huge pressure which made me weep, it was the realisation that, in what seemed to me to be a nightmare, he was feeling terrific! He had a huge smile and was totally relaxed! I was transfixed. Which door had he opened in his head to find such happiness in this nightmare? What did he see in this unfathomable blackness? I do not know what he saw, but he saw it, and that made him terribly happy ...'

11 Besson records this early part of his life in the only official autobiography to date, see Besson (1993) 12, 'I left my soft cotton-wooled dream very brutally'.

could have propelled him into delinquency, drugs and hooliganism. What prevented this was his deep attachment to nature. Elsewhere, in an interview, he talks about the grounding effect of this love of nature: 'living close to mountains and sea gives a solid foundation. It makes you stronger against artificial rules. The rules of society can hurt you but cannot destroy you, because you know that's not what life is about.'[12] This of course is one of the strong messages of his films: that in each and everyone of us, as with his protagonists, there lies a strong inner core, a self-belief that nothing can assail even if it means finding death (as all his protagonists do, literally or metaphorically).

The brutal awakening Besson himself describes – as from a soft dream into a consciousness of loss – forced him to reassess his own future. He was still a boarder at the *lycée* on the boulevard Sébastopol in Paris (where he had been since the age of 9), still a minor, and he had not yet sat his *baccalauréat* exam when he decided to quit everything, school, family and friends, and make his way into the filmmaking business and become a filmmaker. His decision was motivated by two things: first, a personal inventory of his greatest sources of pleasure (beyond the sea and dolphins of course). These were: music, photography, painting, writing and storytelling – all of which to his mind pointed him in the direction of cinema.[13] The second motivating force was his first experience of a film set which left him with two major sensations: the sound of the camera, which to him was like the sound of a beating heart, and the play with/of the actors and the relationship between director, actor and performance. This experience was the *déclic*, the deciding factor: for Besson it was, at 17, cinema or nothing. Henceforth, that was to be his family. He gave himself ten years to learn and understand everything. Amazingly, by the time his deadline of ten years had elapsed he had already made two feature films (*Le Dernier Combat* and *Subway*).[14]

12 Besson quoted in *The Observer Review*, 30.10.94.

13 Besson (1993) 12.

14 For fuller details see interview of Besson in *Première*, no. 134, May 1988, and Besson (1993) 12–14.

Up until this moment, Besson had been a mere filmgoer, like most of his friends, visiting the cinema once a week. Now he attended cinema screenings with a vengeance, going to see movies up to ten times a week. Sometimes he went to see a particular film several times over to see how it was made. He also read extensively about *mise-en-scène* which is doubtless where his good framing eye comes from (even detractors of his films recognise that he is an outstanding *cadreur* – cameraman).[15] This stage of his 'apprenticeship' lasted for a year during which time he saw preponderantly 'bad' films rather than 'good' ones. The good ones, he says, were too absorbing and he forgot to pay attention to technique. Comedies were a pretty staple diet as too were cheap venues, and he would often sit through several screenings at a time. Then it was time to learn about the camera equipment, again through books.

Already, in this earliest period of apprenticeship, it is easy to discern a taste for the popular mixed with autodidacticism. A deep interest in the 'how to' rather than the 'why' of making a film marks these first years – a system of self-teaching that would equip Besson with skills in solving technical problems with considerable brilliance and a determination to resolve difficulties rather than cut corners. This practical curiosity around filmmaking has led to an expertise which has meant that technically it is difficult to fault Besson's films, but it may also be the reason why his films attract the opprobrium of highbrow film criticism. *Cinema Papers* criticises the silliness of Besson's work and goes on to quote Michel Ciment (prominent critic for *Positif*) who argues that whilst Besson (amongst others in the new generation of French filmmakers) may be an avid disciple of Stanley Kubrick and seek to emulate his visceral style, he lacks anything substantial to say. Ciment further argues that Besson

15 Besson (1993, 14) recalls how he came across a 1910 treatise on *mise-en-scène* written by a Russian filmmaker (whose name he forgets) and from which he learnt a great deal. This date would suggest that much of the treatise could have been based on framing and movement within comparatively static frames – since that was one of the major debates of the time. Clearly this date precedes by some ten years all the Soviet School of cinema's discussion of editing, montage and formalism.

seems to believe that instinct is enough and appears deliberately to sidestep, if not despise, an intellectual approach to cinema.[16] Besson makes his position quite clear: he never sought to be a cinephile, he has never set foot in the Cinémathèque (the mecca of cinematic intellectualism and a formidable stronghold of all the great and good in terms of film) – as he says:

> je n'avais pas 'l'esprit' cinéphile, je ne l'ai d'ailleurs toujours pas ... Je n'ai jamais mis les pieds à la Cinémathèque, je n'ai jamais été branché sur cette approche du cinéma. Ce qui m'attirait, ce n'était pas 'les films', c'était les FAIRE ...[17]

We recall also that he firmly believes in confronting the popular with intellectualism and that he constantly signposts his bardic function: 'directors are the modern equivalent of medieval bards. We are obliged to go round the world to tell stories.'[18] Or, as he has also said: 'moi je ne fais pas d'art ni de la culture. Je raconte des histoires. Je me sens davantage conteur.'[19] What is certain is that he does not follow in the tradition of the Nouvelle Vague filmmakers, many of whom (though not all) were avid Cinémathèque goers and intellectuals of the cinema who loved to display their knowledge of film history in their own work through innumerable references and homages to films and directors. And it is perhaps for this reason that Besson warns his viewers and critics against looking for film references in his own work. It is also worth noting that auteurism, which was largely associated with the Nouvelle Vague, was later perceived to be a rather romantic aesthetic because it focused entirely on the filmmaker as *auteur,* as the sole producer of meaning, and glossed over the real complexities of the means of production (production practices).

16 See Scott Murray's article 'European Notes', in *Cinema Papers*, no. 80, October 1990, 3.
17 Besson (1993) 12, 'I did not have a cinephile mentality, and I still do not have one ... I have never set foot in the Cinémathèque, I have never been hooked on that sort of cinema. What attracted me, was not "the films", but to MAKE them ...'
18 Besson quoted in *What's on in London*, 1.2.95, 33.
19 Besson quoted in *Première*, no. 211, October 1994, 70, 'me, I make neither art nor culture. I tell stories. I see myself more as a story-teller.'

This romantic aesthetic is ultimately quite narcissistic – the filmmaker-as-author who scripts, produces and directs his (*sic*) film – and indeed, as if to underscore that narcissism, one of the authorial signs of the Nouvelle Vague filmmakers is their tendency to self-referentiality. Although Besson scripts and produces his films as well as directs them, he does not see himself as an *auteur* but as a *metteur-en-scène* – that is as part of the production practice. Besson works with a fairly constant crew of technicians and group of actors and readily acknowledges their role in the production of meaning in his films. And it is in this respect that he becomes identifiable with the 1930s' tradition of film production as a collective undertaking (mostly associated with the so-called Poetic Realist movement).

Besson does of course acknowledge his influences and what he terms his 'idols' – and has cited films that are the greatest to his mind. In a 1984 interview he mentions *One Flew over the Cuckoo's Nest* (Forman, 1975) and *Network* (Lumet, 1976) as two of the greatest films for him.[20] As for filmmakers he cites amongst the classics Cocteau and Carné (interesting, given their stylised *mise-en-scène* and homoerotic camera work); amongst contemporaries in France he admires filmmakers Bertrand Blier and Jean-Jacques Annaud (another interesting combination given Blier's fierce misogyny and Annaud's love of spectacle); finally, on the international level, he mentions Sidney Lumet, Milos Forman, Roman Polanski, Sam Peckinpah and Warren Beatty. It is unlikely, however, that Beatty still rates amongst his idols given the struggle and legal tussle Besson had with him over *Le Grand Bleu* (see Chapter Two). In a more recent interview, he adds Martin Scorcese (particularly for his technique), Steven Spielberg, Francis Ford Coppola and Stanley Kubrick to the list of filmmakers he admires.[21]

But let us return to 1976 and Besson's dramatic decision to quit school and break into film. His story of how he broke into film makes for fascinating reading, particularly for anyone who has similar ambitions. Besson did not go to film school (he could

20 See *What's on in London*, 9.8.84.
21 Interview in *Première*, no. 211, October 1993.

not get into IDHEC (Institut des Hautes Etudes Cinématograph-iques) since he did not have his *baccalauréat*) but worked his way up from the lowest of menial tasks. He did not even get to that first level by invitation, but rather by subterfuge. He would just walk on to sets and act as if he belonged, ingratiate himself by carrying crates of beer, and simply observe all that was going on. Sometimes camera crew would show him the ways in which cameras could be operated. Other times still, he would pretend to be short-listed as an extra and get on to the set that way. At this early stage, when he did manage to get on to the set officially as a 'gofer' or a trainee (even though it was often unpaid), he recalls how he would willingly bunk down on the set ostensibly to guard over the camera but really so he could just indulge his fascination with it.[22]

During his military service (1977–78), which for him was much like school – all theory and no practice and a period during which he learnt nothing – Besson, judged unfit by the army for any other duty, was assigned to desk duties – this was despite his repeatedly asking to be assigned to the film unit. Being on desk duty gave him plenty of time to write and it is here that he wrote his first scenario for a short film: *La P'tite Sirène*. The storyline, at its most basic, bears certain resemblances to his later full-feature film *Le Grand Bleu* in that it tells the story of a free-diver who eventually lets go of the plumbline and goes off into the deep blue with a siren. Having mobilised several people to work with him, including Patrick Grandperret (a filmmaker and friend of Besson's godfather), he went off to southern Italy, where his father was conveniently working, and set about shooting this ten-minute short. It was shot in black and white cinemascope and it cost him 8,000 francs. But it also cost him, as he himself puts it, a painful lesson in humility. It was, he confesses, 'nul', 'beau mais mauvais' and it taught him that 'quand on n'a rien à dire, on ferme sa gueule!'[23]

Chastened but undeterred in his ambition to be in cinema he decided to set up his own short-film production company, Les Films du Loup, and register his film with the CNC (Centre National de la Cinématographie). But he again came unstuck

22 Interview in *Première*, no. 134, May 1988, 90.
23 Besson (1993) 14, 'when you have nothing to say you shut up'.

when, having raised 50,000 francs as capital to launch his company, he went to the bank. The bank manager responsible for film company accounts politely but firmly refused to allow him to open an account, adding that his projects had no future.[24] How wrong he proved to be! Besson's company, under this name, went on to produce his first two feature films in 1983 and 1985. Later he would add a second production company to his name, Les Films du Dauphin. Besson's name is now firmly associated with money-making films and, since the beginning of the 1990s, he has signed up on the production side in the United States with Warner (their joint venture is called Seaside productions) and with JVC (Victor Company of Japan Ltd).

Between 1978 and 1982, when he started work on *Le Dernier Combat*, Besson continued to gain experience in the film world. He went to Hollywood, where he managed to get into Universal Studios, again as a 'gofer'. But at least it enabled him to observe the American way of moviemaking. He returned to France where he landed different types of jobs, gradually moving up the rungs to first assistant on *Les Bidasses aux grandes manœuvres* (Raphaël Delpard, 1981) where incidentally in his role as casting officer he 'discovered' Jean Reno and gave him a part. He also worked on short films and advertisements. A major breakthrough came with his appointment as director of the second production team on Alexandre Arcady's *Le Grand Carnaval* (1983).[25]

By now he was ready to try his own hand again at producing his own work under his company's name Les Films du Loup. This is when his next lucky break occurred in the form of meeting and befriending the songwriter-singer and cabaret artist Pierre Jolivet. The two of them collaborated on a number of schemes culminating in Besson making a promotional film (*Voici*) for a record single off Jolivet's album that was not doing too well in

---

24 Needless to say, Besson names the bank (1993, 14) and that particular manager must now feel quite distressed at his lack of judgement.

25 During this four-year period he worked on films by Claude Faraldo (*Deux lions au soleil*) and Maurice Pialat (*Loulou*). Faraldo's first film *Themroc* (1972) may have influenced Besson's *Le Dernier Combat* in that it is a futuristic fantasy film without dialogue (as is Besson's first film).

terms of sales. It was during this promotional filmmaking that Besson met Eric Serra, a guitarist and one of Jolivet's musicians. Serra, also a composer, henceforth joined Besson's team and has scored the music for all his feature films. This particular project inspired Besson to try his hand again at a short film. Very much a man who embodies the French concept of *le système D* (someone who always falls on his feet, seizes the moment and turns it to his advantage no matter what the odds), Besson managed to borrow a 35mm camera and shot his eight-minute short in black and white and scope. This film, entitled *L'Avant-dernier*, is really a precursor to *Le Dernier Combat*. Jolivet and Reno are the main protagonists in this sci-fi futurist film of a post-nuclear France which Besson would later turn into the prize-winning full-feature film. Interestingly, *L'Avant-dernier* was submitted to the Avoriaz Festival but met with no success. So again a learning curve for the young and committed filmmaker – that ideas can be rethought and elaborated upon and something 'better' might be produced. In fact, friends had suggested to Besson that the short should be made into a full-length film. The rest, as we know, is history.

Technology and texts

Besson's anti-establishment stance feeds into questions of his cinematic style, unsurprisingly given that he did not go to film school, that he is self-taught and worked his way up through the ranks by sheer determination and implicit self-belief.[26] During the three years after he had left the army and before he made *Le Dernier Combat*, he rapidly absorbed aspects of film technique thanks to the work experience he had on various film sets and the occasional pieces of commissioned work with advertising agencies. A major training exercise, which occurred prior to his shooting his first feature film, was a fifty-minute promotional

---

26 For this reason, those who showed belief in him have received his unreserved support in return. However, those who were more than unhelpful or made his way difficult have been both written into and out of his history (Besson gives full details in his individual books on his films).

documentary on Formula 2 racing cars. This came about thanks largely to his own initiative. He first persuaded his godfather who owned a stable of these racing cars that the latter needed the film to promote his cars, and then proceeded to make it. It was then that he met Sophie Schmit, a young junior film-editor, the first in a line of important women who, in these early years, believed in his ability – the second was the producer Michèle de Broca who helped get *Le Dernier Combat* off the ground, the next as we know was the journalist Michèle Halberstadt. Besson returned Schmit's faith in him and helped her on her way to becoming chief editor. Schmit edited this first film of Besson's and indeed his second, *Subway*.

It is worth making the point here that Besson's first feature film exemplifies much of his relationship to technology and text (which was seen by film critics as an art house *Mad Max!*). He uses what technology he has to hand innovatively, constantly adapting it to his *mise-en-scène* needs. In terms of genre, *Le Dernier Combat* is an unusual choice – given that science fiction does not find common currency in French film history. In terms of technique and technology there are three crucial points to make in relation to Besson's work. These are: the importance to him of scope and lightweight cameras, the stress he places on continuity (textural as well as visual and narrative), and his own perfectionist drive. Getting it right from shot to the edited result means it takes him two years to make a film. This is why, so he says, he intends to make only ten films in all.[27] Besson's brilliance at continuity in shooting is remarked upon by many who have worked with him. Although he uses script supervisors for continuity purposes, his detailed attention to framing – thanks to his earlier apprenticeship – means he can mentally retain his shots from one day to the next, indeed one continent to another. Besson most frequently is obliged to shoot out of sequence. Of his seven films to date, only *Nikita* (1990) is shot entirely in continuity. However, he prefers to shoot as much as possible in this way because he feels it helps

27 Quoted in an interview for the *Evening Standard*, 3.2.95: 'It takes two years to make a film, that is bad enough, but all the energy and thought you need makes it feel like ten years.'

both the narrative and the protagonist's character to develop. For instance the whole of Gary Oldman's performance in *Léon* (1994) was shot in continuity. Arguably, if a film (as it usually is) cannot be shot in continuity, then the most difficult aspect in relation to the impression of continuity is the actors' performance because it is so truncated and made up of a series of takes. Besson sees these difficulties as more complex to overcome than technical questions.[28] He has a special eye for casting and picks actors with an uncanny sense of what will work (as, for example, when he chose Jean-Marc Barr over Christophe Lambert for the chief role in *Le Grand Bleu*, and Jean Reno over De Niro, Pacino and Mel Gibson as the eponymous hero of *Léon*).

All seven Besson films to date have been shot in cinemascope and Besson's commitment to shooting in scope stems from his perfectionism and his belief that it is the only shape to work in. As a first aesthetic reason for this choice he cites camera flexibility. He chooses scope over 70mm (an alternative wide-screen format) because, unlike scope cameras, 70mm cameras are too heavy and make it impossible to obtain the camera angles he wants. Furthermore, the lightweight scope camera allows him to make things go quickly. Once Besson has made his choice of shots, he shoots very fast (on average he makes nineteen shots in one day, whilst most directors work at a rate of eight to twelve per day). His desire to make things go quickly is motivated in part by his desire to be competitive with American action movies which is why his films, whilst abundant in action and violence, are so lacking in excess of explanation. In this respect, Besson goes countersay to the tradition of the French thriller which, historically because of costs and different filming practices, has never been as action-packed as its American counterpart. Another influence, both in relation to diegetic (that is, the whole effect of the narrative) speed and the visual appearance of his films, is the comic strip. Besson is not unlike many of his French contemporaries in being a fan of the *bande dessinée* – virtually a popular culture cult-form in France.

28 In terms of directing, Besson has said: 'le plus dur c'est les rapports humains pas la technologie' ('the hardest thing is not the technology but human relations') – interview in *Première*, no. 134, May 1988, 90.

The comic strip is cut down to the bare essentials of narrative line: one is fully into the action from frame one. And its flattened images are fast-edited together – there is nothing left that is spare. Godard once remarked on how cinema had a lot to learn from the sophisticated fast editing of the comic strip. Besson's films seem to exemplify an understanding of this. *Léon*, for example, is made up of 1,540 shots and lasts 105 minutes. The national average for a French film is 400 shots for the whole film.[29]

Besson also chose scope because it matches his own reading of the mechanics of film – what he calls the interiority of film as a medium, its horizontality and verticality. Unlike the square frame of 35mm or bold rectangular effect of 70mm and wide-screen, the scope frame lies as a strip across the screen. We are very conscious of the horizontal and vertical lines holding the image and we are also supremely conscious of the emptiness/blackness of the screen above and below. Scope has a frieze effect and as such traces new perspectives – not the safe illusionist three-dimensionality of traditional 35 and 70mm, but a flattening or distorting of perspectival space. Volumes, settings get distorted and truncated: the spectator has a sense of 180-degree vision on a horizontal axis but on a vertical axis what is perceived does not seem in logical visual relation to the horizontal. As an example of the scope effect, think about the filming of New York – as Besson had to for *Léon*. Fancy trying to put a vertical city into scope (that is, a horizontal format)! This means clearly that standard assumptions about camera position and angles cannot be made. Thus, Besson's choices were determined by his use of scope and he had to choose, if he was to give any sense that there was a sky and openings, he had to break up heights and lines, find precincts and main arteries that offered these openings, avenues leading to bridges, and perspectives shot from upstairs in buildings.

According to Besson, scope has one further merit over other formats. It alters the relationship of characters to settings. On a horizontal axis spatial relations with scope are more naturalistic, real. However, because scope reduces height and produces a flattening effect, the vertical axis recalls the two-dimensionality of the image and so there is a constant tension between reality and illusion in a scope image. Hence its truly filmic properties to Besson's mind. In more general terms, the play with space and volume is quite different from standard formats – the anamorphic lens which creates the scope effect is after all a distorting lens. In scope-framing there is more of the setting in relation to a character held in the same frame than in a standard ratio format. Thus, in a full or general shot, the setting can seem to overpower or crush the characters. At the other extreme, a one-shot close-up of a person's face can never really fill the frame to the exclusion of all else. However, if it is made to do so, then the effect is one of distortion, even grotesque distortion, especially if it is merely part of a face that is shown in close-up (as in some of the close-ups in *Léon*, for example). Given Besson's reading of the individual in society as lonely, suffering and suffocated, his use of scope, viewed in this context, has both a moral and an aesthetic purpose. But his use of scope also widens the frame, broadens the picture and so it hints at the possibility of escape, of finding a way out. Thus, there is always a peculiar sense of hope at the end of a Besson film even though, paradoxically, there is no happy ending.

Besson has been described as a new moralist of the 1980s and 1990s and as neo-baroque.[30] Part of his new moralism refers to his representation of consumer commodities which are negatively connoted, perceived as signs of death and not of well-being. But this moribund contemporary world-view goes further than that in the Besson 'master-narratives', or indeed is in part an extension of these first signs of death. In Besson's film-world we are presented with the death of Utopia – in effect, the death of the free spirit and free love of the 1970s; society is represented as a force that kills love but sells sex. Sex is everywhere, gone is the concept of pure love which, Besson claims, is the message of *Léon*. And one could argue that *Nikita* at least attempts to advocate unconditional love even though it is an impossibility. In Besson's world we are made aware of the death of the family and the father. The mother is

30 See *Revue du Cinéma/Image et Son*, no. 449, May 1989.

virtually nowhere to be seen incidentally. Families, if they exist, are dysfunctional and the father is almost always absent, impotent or, more interestingly, a menace. This death of the patriarch is no longer the post-68 death of the then President-Patriarch General de Gaulle which was seen as a release from authoritarianism. In Besson's films this feeling of death is a morosity that has accumulated over the fourteen-year presidency (1981–95) held by the ageing and corrupt president-patriarch, François Mitterrand. Finally, Besson's moribund world-view leads us inexorably to witness the death of the hero – a death that is presignified through the death of speech (there is very little talk in a Besson movie, particularly in the mouth of the protagonist-hero).

That then is the alienating context in which Besson's protagonists live. His films speak about the loneliness and suffering of his protagonists, all of whom come from modest backgrounds – and this is part of the appeal of his films to his young audiences, as are the solutions they come up with as a way out of their alienation. Besson's films are counter-texts to the unhappiness and desperate visions of individuals suffocating in an AIDS and nuclear society, a society that is morally corrupt and which excludes all deeply emotional bonds. The way out that Besson's protagonists find is by fulfilling an art-form, be it music, violence, love or free-diving. To a considerable extent the theme of escape is also implicit in this type of solution, but again that is part of the attraction of Besson's films. It is also problematic, of course, as later chapters will go on to discuss, not just because escape means the death of the protagonist but because the fulfilling of the art-form can entail the death of others. What for example is Nikita's art-form? Léon's? Violence or love? And in the end is erasure, self-erasure, a solution?

All of Besson's films have as a central theme escape from the constraints of the social world. Hence the presence in his films of the underworld (literal and figurative) as a major attraction – Besson makes it strange and reveals its strangeness. Thus from *Le Dernier Combat* to *Léon* we see, in turn: Paris in ruins, Paris' métro, the deep blue sea, Paris as part of the State machinery, New York fragmented and defamiliarised, an underworld of 'stolen images'.[31] Neither the city nor the deep blue are characters, no anthropomorphism here. Rather, they are atmospheres balancing out, mirroring or at times overriding the narrative – hence the highly stylised nature of Besson's films for which he is often criticised (but he should take heart, one of his idols, Jean Cocteau, was criticised for exactly the same sort of effect considered an excess by some). In an interview, Besson readily admits his predilection for atmosphere over narrative, at least where his first three films are concerned, adding that *Nikita* is his first film to tell a story.[32] Of course the previous films 'tell stories' but they are not what could be termed plot-led, which is arguably the case for *Nikita*. The interesting point with this particular film, however, is that the décor had to work to substantiate the totally unsubstantiable storyline. Hence the mixture of the baroque and the modern in terms of architecture and design to provide a real but menacing atmosphere for this narrative on State terrorism.

Violence is also part of the stylised effect of Besson's films and is more central to the atmosphere than the narrative, even though it does often appear to act as the diegetic *raison d'être*. In fact, given that violence is one of the art-forms protagonists pursue as a means of self-fulfilment, its representation would be hard pressed not to be stylised, even aestheticised. Besson argues that violence is as much a part of the language of drama as any other aspect, in fact, it is a driving force of life, it is both performance and a dramatic element of the narrative.[33] Besson's films tend to embody violence rather than verbalise it – characters literally are the embodiment or the bodily site/sight of violence: the eponymous protagonist Léon, for example, wraps his body up with guns and grenades and finally self-explodes. Violence is traced within or traced upon the body, characters are the stuff of drama and of strip cartoons (a strong influence on Besson's filmic style). And so, here again, we can perceive this notion of an assemblage/admixture of the ancient (drama) and modern (cartoons) – the one co-existing within the other – which brings

31 Besson (1995) 37.
32 In *Première*, no. 157, March 1990, 82.
33 Quoted in *El Amante Cine*, no. 36, February 1995, 5.

critics to describe his work as neo-baroque. As with the baroque, there is a formalism that encapsulates a truth, an exterior that holds hidden an interior but that is always co-present.[34] To give an evident example, let us take *Nikita*. The eponymous protagonist, Nikita, is the embodiment and the site of inscription of violence: she starts out as a punk-junkie who uses violence to fulfil her needs and subsequently becomes the agent of State violence. Women, as Besson says, are not supposed to feel violent but they do.[35] And within this film we witness the progressive co-optation and crushing of Nikita's embodied violence by the State apparatus, and a gradual rescripting of it from outside of her body (by the State) into the acceptable form of service to the State. The increased aestheticisation of the violence in the film, as Nikita is further and further removed from her target, acts as a formalistic metaphor for the increased sense of alienation as she is inexorably forced out of the picture – erased, punished for her earlier transgressive self. Within this formalised violence is inscribed a truth about the socialisation of women. Violent women are transgressive and must be contained at any price.

The baroque is also about excess: the interior being in far greater excess to the exterior as for example in the architecture of churches; it is also about semblance and illusion, particularly within poetry, but again architecture manifests this through the use of *trompe-l'oeil* and other plays with perspectival perception. The baroque was an earlier manifestation of the postmodern delight and play with different mediums and genres. In all these respects we can place Besson's filmic œuvre. His use of excess does not just limit itself to the visual and formal stylisation mentioned above, but also to his play with and deliberate *bricolage* of film genre. The musical, in its post-1970 sense (*Easy Rider*, 1969; *Tommy*, 1975; *Nashville*, 1975), is intermingled with the thriller, fantasy and science-fiction, grand adventure and romantic comedy. The burlesque is never far from the heroic, illusion from truth. As a bard of our times, Besson tells stories that emanate

34 Baroque poetry or architecture are citeable examples of this exterior/interior idea.

35 *El Amante Cine*, no. 36, February 1995, 5.

from the popular as in the sense of the commonly known – this is why he does not elaborate, nor indeed feels the need to elaborate, upon the story by grounding it in a past: it is there, told in its series of emblematic moments. His audiences know where it has come from. What they wait to see is how its present will unfold. What follows in these chapters are some of those unfoldings and how we can choose to read them.

2

Besson in context

Besson and history

As this book goes to press, Besson's seventh film *Le Cinquième Elément*, has just been released (see Postscript for a brief review). It is worth making the point, however, that his first six films span, almost to the year, the fourteen years of President Mitterrand's double mandate (1981–95). Besson's first feature, *Le Dernier Combat*, came out in 1983, *Léon*, in 1994. Given Besson's stated concerns about and with contemporary society and given that his films reflect this concern, it is worth outlining briefly what these fourteen years of Mitterrandism represented especially for the youth class (or indeed classes), since that is the class that Besson primarily addresses.

In 1981, Mitterrand came to power on a great wave of socialist hope for social reform. But by 1982–83, France was severely hit by economic recession as was most of Europe. Thus, the ideals of socialism (as embodied by Mitterrand and his socialist government) were rapidly replaced by programmes of austerity instead. Unemployment increased in unprecedented numbers, affecting particularly the youth class who, because they lacked either experience or sufficient educational qualifications, found themselves excluded from the workplace (*démunis* and *laissés pour compte* were terms of reference that gained common currency to designate this lost generation). Endeavours to rectify this problem through trainee programmes or by extending education to an ideal figure of 80 per cent of school-leavers obtaining the *baccalauréat* were soon dismissed as cynical attempts on the part of the government to keep the youth class off the unemployment rosters. Students who successfully obtained the *baccalauréat* very soon discovered that their diploma was not an open-sesame to work, nor indeed was their continuing education through to university level any guarantee that employment would be there for them at the end of three or four years of study. The gap between the haves and the have-nots widened and new expressions were coined to refer to the socially deprived: *les nouveaux pauvres* became an identifiable class and was a term used to refer to homeless vagabonds who had not chosen their destitution and who, unlike their earlier and mostly elderly counterparts, were on the whole young adults, male and female.

Faced with the deep unpopularity of his government's austerity programmes, Mitterrand turned his presidential antennae outwards to Europe and foreign policy in general. He became a great champion of Third World Rights, even advocating the abolishing of the so-called Third World debt so that the emerging nations of the African, Indian and Latin American continents could begin to stabilise their economy and build for growth rather than be held hostage to the International Monetary Fund and the dictates of First World economics. His plans for Europe were equally, if differently, ambitious and it is here, arguably, that he was most politically successful. Mitterrand developed France's already strong ties with Germany (first West Germany, until 1989, and thereafter the united Germany), he staunchly defended the Maastricht Treaty, advocated monetary union and a Europe without frontiers. Meanwhile back in France an unprecedented number of financial scandals, affecting highly placed politicians and businessmen – all close allies or friends of Mitterrand – were breaking out in the media. Mitterrand's own unclear history during the Occupation period (1940–44), first as a member of the Vichy Government then as a man of the Resistance, became further muddied by his refusal in 1994 to forego and denounce his friendship with the infamous Nazi collaborator and chief of police, during the Occupation period, René Bousquet.

By the early 1990s, the socialist dream of 1981 was a very dim and dashed memory and the President's emblematic standing as a sign for a *Force tranquille* and a *France unie* (the slogans respectively of his first and second presidential election campaigns), plus his claims to be standing for *la génération Mitterrand* seemed no more than empty mediatic clichés redolent with cynicism and opportunism. To the minds of the electorate that had supported Mitterrand (twice even), the left was definitely dead and the promises for equality unfulfilled. The feeling of disillusionment was matched by the increased cynicism felt by all classes of the electorate and was reflected in the mood and practice of most politicians of the right and the left. The 1980s was a period of progressive disenchantment and depoliticisation. Both the left and the right of the political arena were speaking almost the same centrist language. Only the French Communist Party and the National Front were espousing radical and extreme positions, either to the far left or the extreme right, and managing to attract between them respectively 10 per cent and 14 per cent of the vote in most elections during this period. To the death of the left corresponded, alarmingly, the (relatively speaking) huge rise in popularity of the extreme right in the form of the National Front. The National Front had become a recognised and electable party within the electoral system of France and had, therefore, political legitimacy. To the dream of social reform for all, which launched the 1980s, now corresponded a 'legalisation' of the concept of othering in the form of racism, anti-semitism and other forms of xenophobia as exemplified by the National Front. The National Front – a legitimated party that called for exclusion – gained seats in the political assembly (as deputies to the Assemblée Nationale and as mayors and municipal councillors, etc.).

In all of this, unsurprisingly, the youth class felt itself to be increasingly alienated. The left was no better than earlier parties that had been in power and all politicians were perceived as corrupt and uncaring, so there seemed little point even in voting, in exercising one's voice of dissent. A mood of youth-cynicism prevailed then as it prevails now, which in part serves to explain the great popularity amongst this generation of films that speak to this mood of 'no-hopism'. Furthermore, the world of AIDS, drugs, prostitution (male and female) is one with which the youth class is very familiar. Cyril Collard's film *Les Nuits Fauves* (1992), in which he also starred, has resonances for this class, particularly the protagonist's hedonistic search for pleasure as he is dying of AIDS. This role was embodied by Collard who died of AIDS just before the release of the film. The film met with huge acclaim as did Collard's central performance. The protagonist's cynical advocacy of unprotected sex, his desire to live for the moment and experience as much as possible for that moment is not the message of decadence that certain critics might have tried to impose on this film. Rather, the film speaks to a generation for whom there is little hope for the future. It is a film that may well help to make clear, to those who profess a lack of understanding of this youth generation, why there has been such a poor response to the numerous AIDS campaigns for protective sex. Of all European countries, France has the highest percentage of HIV patients and survey after survey has shown that, AIDS-awareness notwith-standing, the preference is still to have unprotected sex. The individual's freedom to choose, the feeling of *m'en-foutisme* and social malaise are the most often cited sources of this indifference. Although this could be read as a stance around the republican principle of freedom that might for some beggar belief, it should instead be considered for the very real message of despair that it is.

It would be unfair to say that the whole of the Mitterrand era was a failure and that the corruption during his presidencies was any greater than in previous ones. For those who were in the category of the 'haves', for those who were above the poverty and unemployment lines, many social reforms were introduced and benefited their quality of life. The professionalisation of women is one example of progress as too are the improved conditions for child-rearing. Thus the world described above is the more pessimistic political cultural environment and it is one that is not everyone's plight. It is, however, the one that Besson has in mind when he speaks of the emotional deprivation suffered by the youth class. Society, he says, has 'unbalanced the family, creating emotional deprivation in young people'.[1] It is interesting that in that same quote he speaks of the family as unbalanced – as an effect of society. In all his films to date (with the exception of *Atlantis* which is about marine life), the family in disarray is a constant theme: absent mothers, dysfunctional fathers, lone children/adolescents are all visible or invisible signs of this lack of family and social equilibrium. The figures for divorce, broken homes and single-parenting give a relative credence to this concern with the family.[2] But it is also of course the effect of an ageing patriarch – in the form of President Mitterrand – upon a nation's self-image that feeds into the mentality of a society that is ill at ease with itself. Mitterrand's trajectory from a vigorous and modern presidential candidate of the early 1980s to an ageing, terminally ill and fragile end-of-term president of 1995 is not dissimilar to that of General de Gaulle from the late 1950s to the late 1960s. By the end of the 1960s, France's youth galvanised to eject the patriarch from office (the events of May 1968) and eventually De Gaulle did go. What is interesting is that this time there has been no such sustained manifestation of discontent so as to effect or force a resignation – and this would indicate a youth class that senses its disfranchisement. This then is the *génération Besson*, the one to whom his films speak.

Texts and contexts: a synopsis of Besson's films

Le Dernier Combat (1983)

Le Dernier Combat is 'une balade imaginaire' (says Besson).[3] He came to the idea of making this film when he was wandering around in the boulevard Barbès in Paris and came across an old film theatre all gutted out but with cinema seats still hanging off the wall. He thought that there must be hundreds of places like

1 Besson quoted in *The Observer Review*, 30.10.94.
2 It is estimated that the divorce rate is around 35 per cent, single parents stand at 25 per cent of all parents, and that in Paris one in two people live alone (*Insée Première*, no. 482, August 1996).
3 Besson quoted in interview in *Télérama*, no. 1734, April 1983, 29

that in Paris and it was then that he put those sights and thoughts together with an earlier suggestion made by friends that he should make a feature-length film of his short *L'Avant-dernier*. He talked the idea over with his friend Pierre Jolivet and that is how it began. Financing the project was a far more arduous and less spontaneous affair. Besson did not get State funding in the form of an *avance sur recettes*, nor were any of the established producers interested in producing his film. So he decided to produce it himself. To do this he expanded his own production company, *Les Films du Loup*, into a feature-length production company by enlarging the capital base. For financing he turned to friends, family and assorted individuals (mostly not in the production business). The biggest contributor to his film was Constantin Alexandrov, a successful travel agent, whose name appears on the credits as co-producer. The rest of the money he raised through sponsoring.[4] The total budget came to 3.5 million francs (the average cost of a French film in 1983 was 9.5 million). Gaumont, whilst unable to put money forward for production, committed themselves to a limited exhibition of the film. This early belief in Besson by Gaumont has meant that, to date, he has remained with this production and distribution company whilst also maintaining his status as independent producer with his own production companies, *Les Film du Loup* and *Les Films du Dauphin*.

Shot in Paris and in Tunisia (for the desert scenes), *Le Dernier Combat* is the tale of an unspecified holocaust where all seems lost. Survivors of this holocaust have lost the power of their vocal chords as they stumble about in a Paris reduced to ruins and rubble, and surrounded by the sands of the desert. They are constantly on the forage for food and water. Lost then is the power to communicate, as well as the where-with-all to remain alive. Lost too is the possibility of renewing life since this world is at best sparingly populated by men but with barely a woman in sight. Shot in black and white and scope and without dialogue, the film documents the desperate attempt of a young man to escape a gang of evil-doers only to find himself locked in mortal combat with an

4 Besson relates his financial adventures with some relish and venom in his book
   on the film (see Besson (1993) 29–65).

evil marauder (on the rampage for food and sex). The documentary feel given to the film through the use of black and white film provides an aura of realism to this highly improbable tale. This is particularly true of the shots of the underbelly of Paris. The half-gutted buildings, the abandoned multi-storeyed parking lots – the parts of Paris that France's film industry hardly ever shows (including a former EDF (Electricité de France) factory the day before its demolition and the derelict area around rue Vivienne which at that time had been earmarked for the construction of the new Bibliothèque Nationale). The Paris we know and love offered to us over a century of French cinema has typically been the postcard images with which we signify this city to ourselves (Champs Elysées, Latin Quarter, Tour Eiffel, apartment courtyards, etc.). Not so in this film. Besson shows us a Paris ravaged by costly reconstruction programmes that were begun in the boom years of the 1970s and later abandoned as the economy and thus the construction industry suffered the effects, first, of the oil crises in the late 1970s and, then, the recession that hit France in the early 1980s.

But back to the storyline. In a post-holocaust, desolated urban environment surrounded by a desert, a young man (our hero, played by Pierre Jolivet) struggles to survive against the onslaughts of a gang (*la bande du cimetière des voitures*) whose leader has gained control of the meagre water supplies extant in the city. The leader (Fritz Wepper) keeps a diminutive male (Maurice Lamy) in the boot of his defunct car and uses him as a human mole to go down into the sewers to retrieve water. The opening shots of the film show the hero attempting to fulfil his sexual cravings with the aid of an inflatable doll. As protection against the evil gang, he has barricaded himself into an office building in which he is building his means of escape: a basic, single-propellor plane.

He makes his getaway only to crash-land into a forbidden zone. He escapes into a city which is as derelict as the one he had left behind and stumbles across what he takes to be an abandoned hotel. To his delight there is liquor galore to be had. He drinks himself senseless only to awaken to the sound of rain. He runs outside to refresh himself and drink the water but to his astonishment he is deluged by a rain of fish. At this point he encounters the evil marauder (Jean Reno) with whom he has his first sword and hand to hand combat. Although seriously wounded, he manages to escape and makes it to a defunct hospital which is guarded by a solitary doctor (Jean Bouise). The doctor takes him in. In an earlier scene we had seen the doctor barricading himself against the onslaughts of the evil marauder. We eventually discover – as does the hero – that the reason the marauder wants in is because the doctor is 'sheltering', under lock and key in a cell, the apparently only surviving female. As the wounded hero recovers, so the doctor takes him into his confidence and introduces him (slowly) to the woman – clearly with a view to procreation. To no avail. The doctor is killed by a rainstorm of stones (pelted to death). The marauder breaks in, kills the woman and engages the hero in mortal combat. The hero eventually kills him. Making his escape, he returns to his 'home' city, shoots the gang leader and is acknowledged as the new leader. In his new capacity he is introduced to his domain: yet another derelict building (a former Citroën factory). There he encounters another woman, the dead gang leader's jealously guarded prisoner and perhaps the last woman on earth (Christine Kluger). The film ends.

Le Dernier Combat has been compared to a thinking person's *Mad Max* (George Miller, 1979). *Mad Max* is a fantasy film set sometime in the future and where good finally triumphs over evil. The future-scape is composed of derelict cities and desert towns set in the midst of the Australian outback. The film is a parody of American violence movies (cops, guns and road movies) at the same time as it is intrinsically Australian in its preoccupation with car culture and as a playful if violent vehicle for issues surrounding questions of masculinity. If Miller's film is less a thinking person's movie it could be because all the 'baddies' get wiped out by the cop (Mel Gibson); whereas in Besson's movie, the hero takes over the gang once he has killed off the leader. It is also the case that the conclusion of Miller's film lends itself to a moral reading, however parodic (good clean-shaven heroism triumphing over evil), Besson's not at all. But then on issues of masculinity, Besson's men seem no more or less in crisis than usual and the gay subculture hinted at in Miller's film (with Fifi as the chief of police) finds no resonances in *Le Dernier Combat*. There are possible nods to the Miller film in the form of the inflatable doll (Miller's baddies hijack a window-dresser's model) and the fingers necklace around the gang leader's neck (in Miller's film it is a severed hand caught up in a chain). There are some parallels, then, but the comparison seems ultimately unfair and not particularly useful since both films are about social malaise and as such are equally thought-provoking.

Interestingly, George Miller (who scripted and directed *Mad Max*) was the president of the Alvoriaz Science Fiction Film Festival the year that *Le Dernier Combat* won the two major awards (Critics and Special Jury). *Le Dernier Combat* is a sci-fi film which sets out to play with the genre quite wittily and yet which deliberately resists imposing a reading. It is also, as with all of Besson's films to come, one which manages to combine comedy with violence. Thus, for example, the fights (the 'combats') within this film are clumsy but deadly and simultaneously very funny. They parody the idea of chivalrous single combat at the same time as they play on the tradition of the comic strip images of mortal combat between the representatives of evil and good. As with Besson's other films, too, there is no background provided to what has happened nor why; nor is there any cause provided for extraordinary occurrences (such as the raining of fish and, later, stones) – we merely see the effects and how they are dealt with.

Philip Strick rightly makes the point, however, that there does exist a classical narrative line of sorts.[5] The hero 'makes his break from the tribe, proves his manhood and his humanity, overthrows the malevolent and monopolistic tribal chief, and reaps in his turn the rewards of security and marriage'.[6] The elements of chase and escape are also tropes of sci-fi movies as indeed is the notion of the woman as a trophy for the vanquisher. But of course, this is a phyrrhic victory since there are little to no resources left and the

5 See Philip Strick's review in *Monthly Film Bulletin*, vol. 51, no. 607, 1983 239–240.
6 *Ibid.*, 239.

barren desert that surrounds and, moreover, invades the city at times of storms gives every evidence that life is dead. There is then little point in procreation. The Hollywood happy ending has a hollow resonance to it, therefore. Furthermore, the vestiges of humanity referred to above are more than ambiguously played out. The doctor saves the hero's life for his own selfish purpose: he is no longer of an age or physical well-being to be the proper fornicator for the young woman; and it is made clear that his interest in bringing the young couple together is not without voyeuristic intent. The hero, for all that he is sympathetically portrayed, nonetheless kills to stay alive – even though he kills only the baddies – and pure self-interest motivates his pursuit of woman from rubber-doll cypher to another man's captive. Sex is like any other consumer commodity, ultimately replaceable. Sex, like other consumer commodities, lies languishing in death-cells in this film alongside the electronic goods partially submerged under water – all markers of a moribund society that believes in the principle of consumate and consuming egocentrism. Thus, although the title of Besson's film may well refer to the last battle/ stance for humanity – it seems a fairly doomed stance.

Subway (1985)

A few weeks prior to the time that Besson came up with his idea for Le Dernier Combat, he had just completed putting the finishing touches to his scenario for Subway. He had even got so far as to get a producer who, in the end, dropped the project three weeks before it was supposed to go into production. With hindsight, Besson admits that it was as well that he had been obliged to cut his teeth on Le Dernier Combat because he was not really ready for a film like Subway. According to Besson, it was too big and heavy to handle for a first feature film and he is convinced that if he had shot it at the time he made Le Dernier Combat it would have been a flop.[7] The emphasis Besson places on readiness for a project is instructive (not just for all would-be filmmakers). It demonstrates

7 Besson (1993) 37.

Besson's own measure of his abilities. Mention was made in the previous chapter of his resourcefulness, but his capacity to learn from each film venture, not to fall prey a second time to the sharp practices of others, his sense of timing and his commitment to ensemble working and team work are all aspects of his film career that have made him one of France's contemporary filmmaking successes.

After the bleakness of *Le Dernier Combat*, Besson decided to make a lighter film. The project for *Subway* was brought out again and rescripted. Gaumont were very interested in the project as was Isabelle Adjani for whom Besson had just completed making a ciné-clip for her single record *Pull-marine*. Adjani had not made a film for two years so it was a chance for a star role (as Héléna) in a medium-budget film (*Subway* cost 15.5 million francs; the average cost for a French film in 1985 was 11.5 million). Christophe Lambert, although not the first choice for the male lead (originally it was supposed to have been Sting), came hot from his success with *Greystoke* and brought a manic intensity to the role of Fred, the erstwhile musician who has lost his ability to sing (his vocal chords were seriously severed in an accident preventing him from ever singing again). This film, more so than *Greystoke* at least within the French consciousness, spearheaded Lambert's meteoric rise to stardom and brought Adjani back into the limelight. It also launched Besson's career as a bankable filmmaker with mass audience appeal and great box-office potential. Gaumont had made a good investment in producing this film with Besson (who was also a producer through his own production company) and to date that relationship remains.

Before coming to the storyline, it is worth drawing some points out about Besson's mode of work. Over the years, but really as early as *Le Dernier Combat*, he has accumulated a regular but also expanding team of people with whom he works. Carlo Varini has been the director of photography on the first three films, Thierry Arbogast the last three. Eric Serra has been the composer for all films to date. Jean Reno has appeared or starred in all the feature films (except *Atlantis*). Jean Bouise, an established actor with the major film agency Artmedia, made cameo appearances in four of

Besson's films, but died when working on *Nikita*. Pierre Jolivet has been involved in Besson's early career as has Sophie Schmit. His father, Claude Besson, has been involved either as executive producer or actor in all films. And so on. Each film experience leaves its traces from which Besson learns new strategies for production practices. For *Subway*, and just to quote as one example of this learning curve, Besson managed to secure the services of Alexandre Trauner as production designer. Trauner designed the set for the Billancourt métro station in *Subway*. Trauner's career, within French film history, spans back to the 1930s when he designed many of the sets for the films of the so-called Poetic Realist school. Most significantly, within the context of Besson's film, Trauner was the set-designer for Carné's *Portes de la nuit* (1946), an ill-fated film which raised many a controversy not least of which was the huge expense of the reconstruction of the Barbès métro which Trauner designed. The realism of that set was offered then in the 1940s as sufficient justification for the costs in post-war France. The realism of Trauner's studio sets in *Subway* is a remarkable effect of the film as is their clever integration with real locations in the Paris métro. Besson's decision to exploit Trauner's expertise provided the filmmaker with a learning experience that he would be able to draw on when shooting *Léon*, in which he matches sets in Paris with real locations in New York. This ability to match has become a trademark of Besson's work and one that is often commented upon by critics, a conjunctural outcome doubtless of his own brilliance in framing coupled with Trauner's expertise in set-design.

Precision in scriptwriting is another trademark of Besson's work. For *Subway*, the original text was worked on not just by Besson but by several other scriptwriters and at two different stages in its development. First, up until it was dropped in 1981–82 and subsequently when it was brought back into production in 1984–85. In all there were eleven different versions of the scenario.[8] This precision also feeds into his shooting and post-production schedules which are quite long by most film production standards. On average Besson takes three months to

8 *Film Français*, no. 2029, 22.3.85, 8.

shoot a film – time invested, he would claim, to get the results he wants. The shooting of *Subway* took nineteen weeks, fourteen of which were spent in the métro. Post-production on a Besson film (editing, sound track, etc.) can be at least three times as long. Interestingly, since *Nikita*, Besson has been solely in charge of screenplay and adaptation which may account for the greater focus still on action over dialogue. Neither Nikita nor Léon are endowed with length of speech. Indeed, ever since *Le Dernier Combat* speech and control over it, articulacy and inarticulacy have been central themes in his work. Besson speaks of his own experience with language as one who was intimidated to write because he was always being reprimanded for his poor expression in French (which primarily took the form of spelling errors). So, from the age of 16 he started writing in secret (*en cachette*), producing the ideas that eventually got developed into films.[9]

Subway, then, was a slow film to come into being. Besson says: 'j'avais une idée forte: le métro. Mais je n'arrivais pas à trouver une histoire aussi forte que ce décor.'[10] His intention was to create 'un monde aseptisé, un peu intemporel'.[11] And this desire to match story with décor, to juxtapose narrative fantasy with visual realism is a further trademark of Besson's work (one for which he is often chided by French critics in particular). To resolve this problem, he had to resurface and think the storyline through from above ground. Already, then, the script has Orpheic undertones. And one of the ways this film can be read is as a counter-Orpheus narrative because it is Héléna, the woman, who goes down into the labyrinthine underground to find Fred (not as with the original myth, in which Orpheus the poet goes down into Hades to retrieve Eurydice). This inversion of roles on a gender front is reiterated at the end of the film because Héléna looks for and finds Fred and in their exchange of glances it is he, not she, who dies for looking at her. The film is a melange of genres. It is a comic thriller (until the end) and it is also a musical (in the loosest

9 Interview in *Première*, no. 157, April 1990, 129.
10 Besson quoted in *Film Français*, no. 2029, 22.3.85, 8: 'I had a good idea: the métro. But I couldn't find a story that matched the strength of this backdrop.'
11 *Ibid.*, 9: 'an asceptic somewhat atemporal world'.

sense that it relies on a very heavily scored sound track and performances of a diegetic rock-band).

The film begins with a vertiginous car chase from the outskirts of Paris into the city centre. Fred, dressed in a dinner suit, escapes from the car he is driving at break-neck speed into the métro hotly pursued by four men who are similarly sartorially clothed. We learn that Fred had been to Héléna's party and blown open her husband's safe (when he sees a safe, he has to blow it he declares). He has purloined some important documents (possibly incriminating) which Héléna's husband wants back. The husband, incidentally, is played by Constantin Alexandrov, the chief producer of Besson's first film (the role is not exactly a flattering one, he plays the rich possessive husband). Once the initial pursuit through Paris fails, the husband sends Héléna as bait to retrieve the documents, but that backfires. A strong attraction develops between the two main protagonists and eventually Héléna seeks to rejoin Fred in his new world underground. She enlists the help of the métro police who, for their part, are hotly in pursuit of a roller-skater-purse-snatcher (Jean-Hughes Anglade). The chase for Fred has doubled: first, the husband's henchmen and now the police. Fred in the meantime has met up with a motley crew of people who live underground in the métro. He befriends the roller-skater and through him gets to meet people who will help him fulfil one of his ambitions: establishing a rock group. Having lost his own singing voice, he is desperate to succeed by proxy. The end of the film brings success and possible death together as the chase draws to an end. Fred gets his rock-band (which includes Eric Serra as bassist and Jean Reno as drummer) to give a first concert in the métro. The concert is a wild success but Fred lies wounded, shot in the back (by a hit-man), as Héléna runs forward to meet him.

Besson speaks of the people who inhabit the métro in his film and for whom it is their city as 'des personnages fêlés, perdus, des enfants'.[12] These slightly crazed, lost children of the underworld are the ensemble backdrop against which the love story between Fred and Héléna develops. However, these characters are not

12 Besson quoted in *Film Français*, no. 2029, 22.3.85, 9: 'flawed characters, lost, children'.

without their own narratives and dreams – hence the symbolic/ metaphoric value of the success of the band at the end of the film which brings together a number of the secondary characters. As with the community above ground, these métro-dwellers are neighbours, they all know each other and are interdependent; similarly, the métro police function to maintain (however unsuccessfully) law and order below ground just as their colleagues above in the streets of Paris struggle to do. It is the weaving of these various second-order narratives alongside the main one that gives the storyline the depth Besson felt it lacked beforehand. And this type of narrative-structuring is one that is readily associated with the cinema of the 1930s where secondary plot-lines ran side by side with the first because of the casting practices of those times when numerous renowned actors and stars were brought together on any one film and a script was built to accommodate them all.

In this film Besson says that he wanted to show not the violence of the métro but both its sterile side and its more disconcerting and glaucous aspects.[13] The métro, taken as a metaphor for the city as Besson suggests, brings *Subway* close in kind to the intention of the décor of *Le Dernier Combat*: the city of Paris-as-not-beautiful, but as inhospitable, uneasy, sterile but also unclean, unpleasant – in short, not easy to live in. Indeed, violence is less within the métro, but something that comes into it from without. In fact, violence is on a decreasing order of magnitude the closer one gets to the dwellers of the underground city. The husband's hit-men are the brutes, thugs and murderers; the métro police merely brutes and rather ineffectual; as for the métro-dwellers, theft and stealth are the major methods for staying alive in this underground world for those who live in it and mostly the trophies are shared.

Subway's narrative line bears certain resemblances with that of *Le Dernier Combat*. The film is constructed around a manhunt, the themes of chase and escape are there as before as is the notion of the woman both as emprisoned and as trophy – Héléna is caged in (to the point of suffocation as she says) by her husband and the minders he employs. Fred's mission in the film is to escape his

13 *Ibid.*

pursuers, win the woman and fulfil his musical ambition. In effect he does all three – as the ambiguous ending of the film makes clear – but there is no more sense of permanence around his successful trajectory than there is at the end of Besson's first film. Fred has won a moral victory, and the love of the woman he has pursued, but as with the main protagonist of *Le Dernier Combat* there is great improbability that he will live to enjoy it.

Similarly, as with Besson's earlier film, there is a fascination with flotsam, some of which is put to creative use. In much the same way as the costumes of the two main protagonists of *Le Dernier Combat* are cobbled together out of 'recyclable' waste (rubber tyres, electric wires, tin cans, etc), so the roller-skater's underground pad is a *bricolage* of waste material (an old hammock, lilo, venetian blinds, etc.), and the flower-seller-cum-'marchand d'habits' (played by Richard Bohringer) provides an endless supply of recyclable identities with his sack full of old clothes. Food and drink play a significant role in this film as they did in *Le Dernier Combat*. They act as substitutes for what cannot be had – sex, love, the maternal body, yes – but they also signify a nostalgia for an aestheticism, a tradition of value around the consumption of food and drink that has disappeared. The doctor in *Le Dernier Combat* desperately holds on to the niceties of food consumption through his insistence on the formal dinner table. In *Subway*, champagne is consumed with cake at the birthday party where Fred encounters his future underground friends, and again champagne meets up with the traditional baguette in celebrative mode at the impromptu 'surprise-party' Fred has with Héléna and the roller-skater. However, whiskey and *haute cuisine* get a less favourable representation. The sophisticated drink from America becomes an item of tension in this film because it gets stolen from the roller-skater's cache (notably by the flower-seller), and the posh dinner, where Héléna insults her hostess, is dismissed as 'nul'. In the latter case, what is being objected to by Héléna (now she is beginning to find her wings) is the hypocrisy of the bourgeoisie and their anality which, amongst other things, prevents them from truly enjoying food (we see one of the guests prissily removing food he does not like from his plate on to his wife's, declaring repeatedly 'j'aime pas ça'). In the former case, as with earlier *films noirs à la française* (particularly of the 1950s), whiskey – although definitely seen as an attraction (the roller-skater likes to have it to impress his guests) – ultimately measures up unfavourably to the indigenous drink (be it wine, French apéritifs, or champagne as in this instance).[14] The French champagne marks moments of pleasure (birthday parties etc.); whiskey annoyance, displeasure and feeling ripped off.

The critical reception of *Subway* was very mixed. The Anglo-Saxon journals mostly appreciated the film both for its look and its ensemble playing.[15] *Films and Filming* saw links with the work of David Lynch and praised the filmmaker for his brilliant and versatile use of the steadicam and louma camera.[16] Conversely, the French journals criticised it for its lack of realism, and for its lack of topography. It was not, said Michel Chion in *Cahiers du Cinéma*, 'un métro de cinéma', nor did the film give a sense of the Paris métro.[17] Rather, it was a vague 'somewhere' in which no real people existed or lived. Why for example, asks Chion, was there no reaction-shot to the handcuffing of the roller-skater in the métro carriage? And can we seriously believe, he continues, that Fred is both the hard-nosed unscrupulous individual and the sexual innocent he is made out to be?[18] *Positif* and *Le Jeune Cinéma* both disliked the film intensely, seeing it as a degree zero film, as the worst film of the year.[19] Finally, they saw it as a hybrid between the American thriller genre and the French thriller comedy that does not work.

14 Ginette Vincendeau has written very interestingly about this whole issue of ambivalence around Americanness and the *film noir* as it gets played out in French thrillers/*polars*. See Vincendeau, 'France 1945–65 and Hollywood: The *Policier* as Inter-National Text', *Screen*, vol. 33, no. 1, 1992, 50–80.

15 In the 1980s a term 'le cinéma du *look*' was coined and used in reference to the work of Besson and other young filmmakers (particularly Beineix and Carax). As one might expect it is both a descriptive and dismissive term: it refers to the emphasis in the film on the visual, the image seeming to count for everything, and it means that the film lacks in substantive meaning. Guy Austin (1996) gives a useful analysis of this 'cinéma du *look*' in his book *Contemporary French Cinema*, Manchester, Manchester University Press.

16 *Films and Filming*, no. 371, August 1985, 46–47.

17 Michel Chion, 'L'Age du capitaine', *Cahiers du Cinéma*, no. 373, June 1985, 76.

18 *Ibid.*, 77.

19 See *Positif*, no. 292, June 1985, 79, and *Jeune Cinéma*, no. 167, June 1985, 44–45.

With *Subway*, Besson claims that he deliberately did not go for identifiable métro stations but that he wanted to re-create the métro more as a space-station and focus on form and colour rather than direct realism. He did shoot on location, however, and Trauner did re-create Billancourt in the studio and there is, therefore, an authenticity to the environment: we do recognise the idea of the Paris métro system; but we also see it as an unfamiliar space particularly the underside of the métro, the hidden métro where a whole *demi-monde* lives and breathes. The métro becomes a labyrinth that fascinates in its familiar unfamiliarity. Furthermore, the métro is a meeting place for the *génération Besson*. Young people do meet there and do deals there and they do get stopped by the métro police and harassed by them. And it is in this respect that the characterisation of Fred is, ultimately, 'believable'. The young are a mixture of the tough, the street-wise and the inexperienced. So there is pleasure in identification for them and there is also, of course, pleasure in seeing the police outwitted and outplayed by the young. And some of the funniest scenes in the film are those dealing with the bureaucracy and stupidity of the police – a very old convention of the French thriller-comedy.

There is no question that *Subway* is a hybrid genre. It cuts across the thriller, the comic-thriller, the musical and fantasy. But this is nothing new: the Nouvelle Vague was one such film movement whose films deliberately mixed genres with a view to questioning genre fixity (codes and conventions). Besson's hybridisation of genres is doubtless more playful than counter-cinematic (as was the case for the Nouvelle Vague); and it could be argued that what emanates is a *bricolage* of genres, an exercise in style rather than any deliberate polemic about cinema. But Besson's purpose is to address a specific if broad-based audience with a particular set of concerns. His films act as empowerments for those who feel marginalised, disfranchised. They are therefore visually very exciting. However, they consistently end in a form of realism, sobering realism: his stories do not have happy endings – in this instance, the love story. His films are also hybridisations of cultures. We know that Besson himself has declared that he wants, with his films, to cross-fertilise between American and

French cinema – to bring the speed and action of Hollywood into line with narrative structures that are French. In the final analysis, the very strength of Besson's cinema, which may well alienate the purists, is its intertextuality. His cinema refers back to the 1930s and the Nouvelle Vague, it also refers to Hollywood and – as an end product – to contemporary production practices.

Le Grand Bleu (1988)

It was whilst making *Subway* that Besson got wind of the fact that Jacques Mayol had broken the 100-metre barrier. Mayol was the free-diver whose exploits Besson had first heard about in a documentary he saw in 1976. At that time, Besson had been forcibly struck, not by the feat of free-diving itself, but by the perceptible effect it had had on Mayol's body and persona. He telephoned Mayol in Marseilles who invited him to come down and talk. For Besson, this was the beginning of a dream that might come true. What came out of that dream was the film *Le Grand Bleu*. This film is a homage to Mayol, it is also a salutation to a career that Besson would never have, and finally it is a dedication to a life almost lost: that of his daughter, Juliette, born during the making of the film but who had heart problems and had to be operated on three times as a newly born infant.

All three references are to lives that were in some way at risk, close to death. When Besson first saw the documentary of Mayol's free-diving, he describes the plunging into the deep blue as follows:

> Mayol longe le Bleu comme un oiseau longerait une vague, puis il quitte le bleu et glisse vers la nuit … J'ai l'impression d'assister à un suicide en direct, tellement tout cela me paraît à la fois fou, violent et incroyablement délicieux … Mayol arrive à quatre-vingt-douze mètres … je ressens un choc énorme … : Le visage de Mayol est … radieux.[20]

20 Besson (1994) *L'Histoire du Grand Bleu*, Paris, Intervista, 15. 'Mayol swam along the sea like a bird would a wave, then he quit the blue sea and slipped into the night … I had the impression that I was watching a suicide on live TV, because everything seemed so crazy, violent and delicious all at once … Mayol reached 92 metres … I felt an enormous shock …: Mayol's face was … radiant.'

Once safely back at the surface, it is as if he does not want to be there, says Besson: 'au fond de son regard, il y a de la tristesse. La tristesse d'être à nouveau parmi nous'.[21]

It was both the radiance and the regret that Besson wanted to understand. But, as already mentioned in Chapter One, Besson had had a diving accident when he was 17 and had been forbidden ever to dive again. He conveniently decided he had been told only not to go scuba-diving. So, defying doctor's orders he set about gaining first-hand experience of free-diving. This is how he describes the sensations (the year is still 1976):

> L'eau a glissé sur mon visage, comme un vent doux et lent. Une caresse. Descendre ainsi est d'une sensualité que je ne soupçonnais pas ... Après vingt-cinq secondes d'une magnifique descente, les yeux fermés, le bout se tend et me stoppe en douceur. Je suis à trente mètres. Au-dessus ... je ne vois plus la silhouette du bateau ... En-dessous, le bleu, Le Grand Bleu. Plus un bruit. Plus de pesanteur, plus de drame, plus rien. Je me sens tellement bien que j'ai l'impression d'avoir de l'air pour des siècles. Je lâche le bout pour me sentir encore plus libre et j'ai lentement la sensation de disparaître, d'être nulle part et partout à la fois ... Je me sens 'eau', je souris, je suis bien. Je pourrais rester là. Je veux rester là. En fait, je suis tranquillement en train de me noyer.[22]

The third near-death refers of course to the far more real circumstances surrounding his daughter, Juliette, to whom the film is dedicated. Besson is sparing with the details (typically, he is very private about his personal life). However, for three weeks she hung perilously between life and death. She survived the operations

21 *Ibid.*, 16, 'deep in his eyes, there was sadness. The sadness of having returned to us.'
22 *Ibid.* 'The water slipped over my face, like a slow and soft wind. A caress. To go down this way has a sensuality I never imagined ... After 24 seconds of a magnificent descent, my eyes closed, the rope end brings me softly to a halt. I am 30 metres down. Above ... I can no longer make out the silhouette of the boat ... Below, the blue, the deep blue. Not one sound. No weight, no drama, no nothing. I feel so good that I have the impression that I have enough air for centuries. I let go of the end of the rope so I can feel even more free and I experience the slow sensation that I am disappearing, that I am nowhere and everywhere all at once ... I feel like "water", I smile, I feel really good. I could stay there. I want to stay there. In fact I am slowly drowning myself.'

and, after a further operation a year later, went on to lead a normal life. Besson makes no mention of Juliette's mother, Anne Parillaud, during all this trauma but he does speak about the effects of this 'death-experience' on his work. It was a 'tragédie qui a changé toute ma perception du tournage et du film, jusqu'à sa sortie'.[23] In other words, almost the entire shooting and post-production of this film was coloured by this event. Shooting began in late May 1987 and Juliette was born in early June. The last shot was in the can on 20 January 1988. Five months later it was edited and presented at the Cannes Film Festival as the opening film on 10 May, the very day Juliette was due to undergo her further operation. The operation was postponed until the 14th and was a success. However, the film met with the opposite fortune and was panned for its length, its pretentiousness, its cost (75 million francs) and its utter tedium. It looked set to be dead and buried and would have been had not the youth audiences decided otherwise. By word of mouth it became a cult film and Blue-mania took off in a big way. It ran for three years in France and grossed 10 million spectators. Overseas it netted just over four million viewers.

The death and life of the film was not only closely attached to that of Juliette's, it also went through its own serious pre-production problems which might have prevented it ever being made. It is worth briefly detailing these issues since it was a learning experience for Besson in the domain of international film productions. In the very early stages of pre-production when the script was not even yet written, Besson found himself locked in a peculiar log-jam of American production rights which took several months to unravel. Isabelle Adjani, knowing that Besson needed big money to finance his dream project of *Le Grand Bleu*, used her international profile to arrange a meeting between Besson and Warren Beatty. After shooting *Subway*, she was due to work on a Beatty film (*Ichtar*). Beatty, intrigued by Adjani's latest role in Besson's film, asked to see a preview of *Subway*. After seeing the film, Beatty posted $25,000 towards production costs of Besson's next film (*Le Grand Bleu*). And it looked as if Beatty

23 *Ibid.*, 63, 'a tragedy that changed my whole perception of the shooting and the film, until its release'.

with 20th Century Fox, or maybe Warner Brothers, would be part of the producer-package alongside Gaumont and Besson's own production company. Beatty affirmed he would sort out the contract with Fox. But, because of the American input, the film would be shot in English. Besson looked all set to make the film. Or so he believed.

Beatty kept delaying, saying the script needed reworking. By this time, Besson wanted to pull out of any international project and do the film in collaboration with Gaumont only. However, it soon transpired that, unbeknown to him or indeed to Isabelle Adjani who had tried to help, the production rights had been sold to Warren Beatty as part of a package deal by Adjani's then agent Marjorie Israël. Technically and legally the film was Beatty's to produce. And he could hold off production for as long as it suited him. There seemed no way out of the impasse. Legal wrangles began. An already expensive production looked like escalating massively. But Gaumont stood by Besson. Gaumont's Director, Nicolas Seydoux, had read the script and greatly liked it so he became the force behind Patrice Ledoux (the producer from Gaumont who deals with Besson's films) to push for a resolution. Eventually, thanks to a legal loophole, Gaumont and Besson managed to free the rights away from Beatty and Besson went ahead with his dream, financed to the tune of 80 million francs by Gaumont and Les Films du Loup. Besson's entanglements with the American film industry did not end there, however. The rights to distribution were sold to Fox. Once the film was ready for release in the United States, Fox insisted on cutting a further twenty-two minutes from the already abridged version released in France: its full length is 162 minutes, the abridged version 136, the American version 114. Fox also replaced Eric Serra's original score with one by Bill Conti. Unsurprisingly, the film flopped with American audiences. But the lesson was learned. In future, Besson would be very sure to have all the cards in his hands when making production and distribution deals with the American film industry.

In the light of the above saga, the difficulties Besson experienced around casting appear quite small. The major problems concerned the two central protagonists, Jacques and Johana. Besson had considerable trouble finding the right people for the roles. He had originally thought of Christophe Lambert for Jacques, then Mickey Rourke showed keen interest. But Besson decided against both, finding them too attached to the earth to act convincingly as 'acquatics'. In the end, he found the perfect dolphin in Jean-Marc Barr. Given Besson's usually very good eye in casting, of the two roles, it was the other one that came as a surprise: the choice of Rosanna Arquette for Johana. Having seen her play in *Desperately Seeking Susan*, Besson was convinced she was right for the role. The ordinary spectator might be forgiven for thinking that she was imposed from outside, but such is not the case. Besson thought she was perfect for the part. However, her performance simply does not gel with that of Jean-Marc Barr's Jacques. The part itself is simply not convincing, even in the full-length version. The biggest failing of this film was the introduction of a love dimension into the intriguing story of why men are transformed once they get into the deep blue and how one man in particular, Jacques Mayol, was born a man and not a dolphin. But before getting into these sort of discussions here is the storyline in brief.

The film opens in black and white in the form of a flashback that establishes the long and deep-seated friendship and rivalry between Enzo Molinari and Jacques Mayol as young boys. It also establishes the idea that the sea is an awesome space that contains the magic of dolphins and the mysteries of death – Jacques's father (played by Besson's own father Claude) drowns in a fishing accident which the young Jacques witnesses and which haunts him until his own death. The young Jacques is played by Besson's half-brother Bruce Guerre-Berthelot. In relation to a theme constant to all Besson's films – the family – this flashback also functions metonymically for the precarity and instability of the patriarch within that particular institution. Indeed, how else to interpret the fact that by the end of the film three men have been claimed either by dolphins/sirens or the sea/*la mer* herself?

Molinari (Jean Reno) grows up and becomes the world free-diving champion. Jacques pursues more esoteric work in the form of freelance diving for scientific purposes. Enzo's competitive spirit cannot rest, however, until he has proved to himself that he is better than Jacques. So he lures Jacques back from Peru where he is doing high-altitude diving experiments, but not before Jacques has encountered Johana, an insurance investigator from New York, who has been obliged to come to the Peruvian research centre where he works to evaluate an insurance claim. Smitten, she finds a way of following Jacques to Sicily where a free-diving championship is to take place. Jacques wins, thus setting in motion the drama of rivalry that will lead to his and Enzo's death. Jacques is always the reluctant but nonetheless 'willing' participant in this rivalry. Just as the deep-sea affair develops so too the land love-affair gets underway. Jacques eventually succumbs to Johana's charms and they make love (with Johana on top). But only briefly. He slips out after making love and frolics in the sea with a female dolphin. Johana, sensing the sea and the dolphin as her rivals, now becomes obsessed with having a baby by Jacques – as a way of holding him to the land. Again Jacques succumbs. In this second love scene with Johana, Jacques is on top, but he hallucinates himself swimming naked up to the camera eye – a possible forewarning that he is betraying his true love. Whatever the case, the deep-sea affair grows apace and Enzo determines to beat Jacques's record in a world-diving competition. So the two set about intensively practising. The day of the competition Enzo dives to 115 metres, Jacques goes further (120 metres). Enzo dives again, against all advice to break the record set by Jacques. When he does not return, Jacques dives down to rescue him and brings him back to the surface. To no avail, Enzo dies in his arms and Jacques returns him to the sea, heartbroken at the loss of his friend.

Ordered to rest, Jacques then has a second hallucination, this time in a dream. The sea comes into his bedroom to reclaim him. He awakens and makes for the sea. Johana tries to retain him, telling him she is pregnant with their child. But he is compelled to return to the sea and to the dolphin waiting there for him in the depths of the deep blue.

By all accounts, *Le Grand Bleu* came in 5 million francs under budget, yet it was a colossally expensive film to make. The average cost in 1988 for an all-French film was 15.38 million francs. Besson's film cost nearly five times that. The 75 million francs cost was mainly due to the expense of location shooting and to the design of lightweight underwater cameras. Besson needed the cameras to be light, easy to handle and able to shoot in scope. Nothing like this existed in terms of underwater cameras. Besson unearthed three men, Christian Petron, Marcel Rousseau and François Laurent, and between them – in ten months – they came up with the required technology: two lightweight cameras, both scope, one with a 32mm the other with a 50mm lens.

As for the issue of location shooting, since the film was based on Jacques Mayol's life, Besson felt justified in the varied locations he had to use: the Mediterranean, the Greek islands, the Virgin Islands and Peru. Here is how Besson records his interview with Mayol when he first went to meet him in Marseilles:

> il a plongé dans des lacs péruviens, à près de six mille mètres d'altitude, il est tombé amoureux d'un dauphin dans un aquarium italien, qu'il essaye de racheter ... En attendant, il s'est procuré des hydrophones et lui passe de la musique classique sous l'eau, pour qu'il ne s'ennuie pas trop! Son rêve à lui, c'est d'abandonner la gueuse et de descendre, entraîné par ce dauphin.[24]

In essence these exploits are the skeletal storyline of *Le Grand Bleu*, but the last comment recalls Besson's very first film *La P'tite Sirène*. The rivalry between Jacques and Enzo in the film was based in the real-life rivalry between Mayol and Enzo Maiorca during the 1960s. Curiously the film was banned in Italy, and it is unclear whether it was the stereotyping of the Italian matriarchy or the representation of Maiorca that brought about the ban. One would have expected the Japanese to be far more offended by the quite gratuitous stereotyping they are subjected to in the last, fateful, free-diving competition, but the film was quite a hit there (half a million entries). Mayol is credited as part of the team of scriptwriters who adapted Besson's original idea to screen.[25] The film then is a mixture of fact and fiction, biography

24 *Ibid.*, 30, 'he had dived in Peruvian lakes, at close on 6,000 metres of altitude, he fell in love with a dolphin in an Italian aquarium that he tried to buy ... In the meantime he purchased some hydrophones and played classical music to the dolphin so he did not get too bored! His personal dream was to let go of the weights and to go down carried off by this dolphin.'

and fictional narrative, documentary and feature film. It also contains a strain of autobiography, since Besson is also deeply attached to the sea and to dolphins, and of all his films this is his most personal. Arguably, it is the more factual side of the film that works – and this includes the buddy-relationship between Enzo and Jacques. But as a hybrid between sea-documentary, biography and love-story the film does not hold together.

This issue of failed hybridisation can possibly be explained at the level of the script. As with previous film scripts, *Le Grand Bleu* was rewritten numerous times and was worked on by a number of writers including Marc Perrier who had worked with Besson before on *Subway*. More significant in the context of this film are the American scriptwriters: Robert Garland and Marilyn Goldin. For the record, Goldin, a friend of Adjani's, worked on the *Camille Claudel* (1988) script and Garland, a veteran in television comedy writing, also had to his credit *The Electric Horseman* (1979) and *No Way Out* (1986). Philip Strick suggests that Garland's input into Besson's film could explain, among other things, the dismissive treatment of the heroine and the awkward outbursts of broad humour.[26] As for Goldin's input, Besson says that under her influence the script took on too much of a literary turn.[27] What this suggests is that the real story, the buddy-movie, was padded out by other elements that did not really belong to the essence of the plot. As someone famously says in Robert Altman's brilliant spoof on Hollywood, *The Player* (1992), the script they are planning is '*Out of Africa* meets *Pretty Woman*'. In Besson's case, given the literary dimensions and the length, it could be a case of '*Gone with the Wind* meets *Butch Cassidy and the Sundance Kid*' (or more flippantly: *The Misfits* meets *Flipper*).

In May 1988, *Le Grand Bleu* opened the 41st Cannes Film Festival (unkind rumours had it that Besson set an ultimatum that either his film opened the festival or he would not come[28]). It was

25 We recall that in Besson's film, the dolphin is returned to the sea from captivity. The owner of the dolphinarium is played by Constantin Alexandrov, Besson's first producer.

26 See Philip Strick's review in *Monthly Film Bulletin*, vol. 56, no. 662, 1983, 74.

27 Besson (1994) 35.

28 *Ibid.*, 105.

pilloried by critics and the audience that saw it. The music was too invasive,[29] the film too slow, the characters lacking depth, they said. Why open the festival with an English version of an all-French film subtitled in French? Criticism was also levelled at the secrecy surrounding its screening. There was precious little pre-release information for journalists, and Gaumont (the production company) did not want the film entered for competition. All this was interpreted as hype; which it may well have been. But it is worth remembering that shooting finished at the end of January and there were less than five months to edit it, mix the sound track and get a French version done. From Besson's own records, it was Gaumont that wanted to open the Cannes Festival with his film and the pressure was simply enormous.[30] They were so close to the wire that there simply were no decent copies to show to the press. Everything had to be ready for the Festival and for general release the next day all over France.

The film, despite its critics, became a cult movie. And it was perceived as a New Age movie. The 1980s was a decade of yuppies, greed and an attitude of 'I'm in the money'. New Age people emerged as resisters to this philosophy of get rich quick and hang everyone else, to what could be termed the shark mentality. In this New Age environment, concern for ecology developed, including an intense interest in dolphins whose life-style was seen as an antidote to ruthless profiteering. This burgeoning interest even produced a business studies book entitled *Strategy of the Dolphin*.[31] As an antidote to greed and graft, then, the film has a strong message to deliver.

Atlantis (1991)

Although *Atlantis* was released after *Nikita*, and although it was very much a refuelling exercise and an attempt to go forward in a

---

29 Interestingly it won a César (France's equivalent of the Oscar) in 1989 for best musical score.

30 *Ibid.*, 96–97.

31 Dudley Lynch and Paul L. Kordis (1988) *Strategy of the Dolphin*, New York and London, Hutchinson Business Books.

different experimental vein after the technical and methodological demands of *Nikita* and its precedents, it is more logical to place it here since shooting on it started in 1988 and was completed in 1991. It is also more logical to discuss it here since it can be perceived as a sequel to *Le Grand Bleu* because it continues with the theme of ecology touched upon in the earlier film. Finally, I shall touch on this film briefly and only in this chapter because it is more of a medium-length documentary-opera than a feature film and it is Besson's feature work which is the focus of this study.

Atlantis is a homage to the flora and fauna of the underwater world but it has a polemical function in that it focuses on marine life threatened with extinction. The title is clearly not innocent: Atlantis refers to the large island civilisation, somewhere off the Straits of Gibraltar, that was destroyed by earthquake and sunk without a trace – a natural disaster that removed an entire civilisation. In modern parlance, Atlantis refers to the idea of the lost island, lost utopian civilisation. Thus, Besson is reflecting in this film his fear for the ecological state of the planet, the lost Atlantises human kind is in the process of creating. It is a film, as Robert Yates points out, that takes to task human abuse against the planet.[32] But, beyond the polemical intention of the film, Besson also intended to create an underwater opera. So the film is intentionally not a documentary about marine life in the style of Jacques Cousteau (some French critics saw the film as a 1991 version of Cousteau's *Le Monde du silence*[33]). Besson shot the film with Christian Petron, the man responsible for designing the cameras for *Le Grand Bleu*. And it was filmed over three years in seas all over the world. The music score, by Eric Serra, complements the movements of the various elements of sea life that Besson films. Some sequences are speeded up (as with the seals dance) as a deliberate strategy to move away from under-water documentary. And the other obvious evacuation of any documentary convention is the lack of voice-over. Documentary convention is replaced by *bricolage*. Music and film genre are brought together in playful pastiche as camera work, editing and music-score act in

32 See Robert Yates' review in *Sight and Sound*, vol. 3, no. 11, 1993, 37.
33 For example, *La Revue du Cinéma*, no. 475, 1991, 68.

counterpoint in this witty and at times quite majestic film. The sequence with the mantra ray accompanied by Maria Callas singing Bellini's *La Somnambula* is a stunning piece of counter-pointing, giving beauty to a fish-form that human beings might ordinarily reject as ugly. The rays move like birds, like huge bats, with their front fins held like the sleeved arms of a female opera singer. Bellini's soprano arias are notoriously difficult to sing, requiring singers of outstanding ability to meet the demands of the elaborate and decorative passages (known as *colatura*). The music tells us something about the complexity of this huge aquatic phantom, retains them as awesome and magnificent. The music, camerawork and editing give varying rhythms to the different episodes. In some, the camera gyrates round and round (as with the seals), the music varies from pop, disco, to oriental (for the brilliant sea-snake episode), to cantatas, requiems and high opera. The music and camera also inscribe these episodic moments into ideas of genre, almost as if sea-life is being anthropomorphised through film genre – so that it can be explained to us in terms of reference we can understand. Thus, the giant octopus is inscribed into the thriller and science fiction genre; the killer shark enacts the truth of all those *Jaws* films. At times a terrestrial noise, such as the sound of human voices (for the shipwreck episode), overlays the images as a way of familiarising this unfamiliar world.

Nikita (1990)

Nikita was Besson's thank-you film to his audiences for saving *Le Grand Bleu* from oblivion. This film was, according to the press, released in a shroud of secrecy (much like *Le Grand Bleu*). However, Besson wanted to privilege his public, not the journalists. Thus, he argued that the film should go out on general release and not be premièred for special audiences such as the film critics.[34] This attitude did not endear him to a great majority

34 Instead he invited some 800 people and their partners who had written to him in support of *Le Grand Bleu* and the film was premièred at the Grand Rex in Paris. In all, 2,000 people came and this figure included some 300 journalists. See Besson (1992) *L'Histoire de Nikita*, Paris, Bordas et fils, 174.

of the reviewers. However, as before, his new film was a great success with audiences (it netted a 3.7 million audience in France alone, 3 million in the USA).[35] Critics reproached him for playing guru ('porte-parole') to the youth audience. *Positif* accused him of adopting the role of spokesperson for the young, even of having taken them hostage and of practicising a racism of exclusion when he declared in an interview that the spectators who went to see his film did not need an explanation as to how or why Nikita became a punk-junkie – they knew already – but that those who might need one were their parents.[36] Besson also answers these criticisms by saying that he makes films for 'un public' not 'le public' and by affirming that if his films are popular it is because the audience knows that he does not cheat and that he is not trying to sell them anything in particular.[37]

By not cheating, Besson means that he does not cheat on the shots. The most difficult of shots will not be an easy special effects 'cop-out' but a genuine attempt to create the desired effect through skilful and inventive camera work and 'honest' use of special effects. Indeed, he has the following to say in relation to *Nikita*:

> il n'y a aucun trucage au montage dans *Nikita*. Au contraire, je souhaitais justement faire un film d'action où tout serait fait en direct, sans trucage. Les coups de feu, les impacts, tout a été fait au tournage en direct, parce que cela donnait une authenticité au film.[38]

The famous waste-chute scene in *Nikita* is a good example in this context. The camera had to follow Nikita and the flame-projector down the waste-chute. The chute was an 8-metre high structure

---

35 And in the first weeks of its worldwide release it netted nearly 4 million spectators.

36 See Michel Ciment's review of *Nikita*, in *Positif*, no. 350, 1990, 43–44.

37 See Besson (1992) 173; and the interview with Besson in *Première*, no. 157, 1990, 83.

38 *Ibid.*, 164, 'there are no gimmicks in the editing of *Nikita*. On the contrary, I wanted simply to make an action film where everything was shot live, without any tricks. The gun shots, the impacts, everything was shot live, because that gave a real authenticity to the film.'

and the camera was tied to a rope and placed in a frame with rollers so that it could run down the chute and remain stable. The camera weighed eighty kilos so it was fairly important to get the measurements right or it would have crushed the stuntwoman substituting for Anne Parillaud. The scene was filmed in a single shot (that is, a continuous take) and demanded great synchronisation: first the woman flying head first down the chute, followed by the flames and then the camera.[39]

Getting the project of *Nikita* up and going was far less difficult than *Le Grand Bleu*. In fact, it was thanks to the huge success of this film that Gaumont agreed to finance *Nikita* without even having seen a script. *Nikita* cost 39 million francs (the average for 1990 was 20 million) and was a Franco-Italian co-production between Besson's own company (Les Films du Loup), Gaumont and Cecchi Gori Group Tiger Cinematographica. The actual shooting, as with all Besson films, was a more complex issue. Besson decided that he needed to change his technical crew in order to meet new challenges. After three successful films with Carlo Varini as director of photography, he chose to move on and work with Thierry Arbogast. Both men are interested to see what effects they can produce with light. Both like natural light and simple lighting and this liking had considerable impact on the look of *Nikita* which does demarcate it visually from Besson's earlier films. Because Besson wanted a fairly weak lighting effect, there were problems with shooting in focus beyond a certain length. After one and a half metres there was a loss of depth, and consequently much of the film was shot in medium close-up shots. Given that the film is in scope, this means that the image is very strongly up against the screen in terms of spectator perception – affording the image a certain inherent violence of its own.

In terms of the music, as always, Besson stayed with Eric Serra, even though he did not particularly like the score to the opening credits of the film.[40] To his mind a good pairing of musician to filmmaker is essential: one is the ears, the other the eyes. And, in terms of casting, to his unofficial ensemble of players (Reno,

39 *Ibid.*, 138.
40 *Ibid.*, 165.

Anglade, Bouise) he added the talents of Tchéky Karyo (a choice not liked, initially, by the producer at Gaumont, Patrice Ledoux). This commitment to a stable team of colleagues as well as an ability to forge new alliances are Besson's way of setting himself new goals but sustaining his own sense of a cinematic family. It recalls Renoir's working practices and those of two of Besson's mentors of the classic age of French cinema, Jean Cocteau and Marcel Carné.

Nikita did not meet with much critical acclaim in France. But it was a huge success with French audiences. The Americans, therefore, were very keen to buy up the rights. However, for its release in the United States, Gaumont wisely decided to handle the sale of distribution rights separately from the film rights. The distribution rights were sold to Columbia Pictures and later the rights to the film were sold to Warner Brothers who were responsible for the remake of *Nikita* (released as *Point of no Return* a.k.a *The Assassin*). In other words, the various package deals were far more on Besson's terms than had been the case for *Le Grand Bleu*. He held on to the possibility of shooting the American remake, not because he wanted to make it but because he wanted to be party to the rewrite so that he could see how Warner would americanise his story.[41]

Nikita was the first scenario Besson scripted by himself without his usual entourage of scriptwriters. He wrote it when editing *Le Grand Bleu* and for the first time had someone definitely in mind for the lead role, Anne Parillaud. Generally speaking, Besson chooses actors after the script is written, otherwise he feels he runs the risk of writing for actors and what they are capable of. He wants his roles to challenge his actors (Reno, for example, was terrified of his role as Enzo in *Le Grand Bleu* and briefly went into hiding). In fact, with the role for Parillaud, he wrote very much against type and she had to work hard to embody the persona of Nikita. Interestingly, there are parallels between the *Nikita* narrative and Parillaud's own circumstances at the time. In the early 1980s, she was propelled into stardom thanks mostly to

41 *Ibid.*, 89. In the end John Badham directed it. Besson felt it stayed fairly close to the original except for the ending (a happy one).

working opposite Alain Delon. But, in substance, as she herself says, there was nothing there other than an image constructed by others.[42] She decided in 1983 to drop out of the movie scene. Two years later, Besson asked to meet her and told her flat out that he did not like the roles she had been playing, but felt that she had substance beneath the public image. He promised to write something for her. Three years later, he did, the part was Nikita.[43] When the film was released, Parillaud went from bimbo-starlette to ferocious androgyne to lethally armed female – she was no longer 'Delon's girl'. Press release after press release commented on the fact that Besson had become her Pygmalion and transformed her. 'La douce comédienne sans caractère remarqué devient une zonarde de choc puis une Mata-Hari irrésistible.'[44] And, as if to confirm this regeneration, she won the 1991 César award (the French equivalent of the Oscar) for the best actress. Earlier, in 1990, she had won Italy's Donatello award for best foreign actress. The film itself won best foreign film award at the same ceremony.

Besson was pleased to have acted as her Pygmalion ('j'étais fière de jouer à l'écran son "Pygmalion"'[45]). As for Parillaud she has the following to say about her transformation: 'Nikita cassait cette image de poupée que les gens ont de la femme (...) ça cassait toute cette image que je traînais derrière moi.'[46] Indeed, Nikita did help to relaunch her career – very much on the international scene – since she went on to make in rapid succession The Map of the Human Heart (Vincent Ward, 1992, GB/Austr/Fr/Can) and Innocent Blood (John Landis, 1993, US). However, it was a curious Pygmalionisation of Parillaud since she was trained up in the opposite vein of lady-likeness and good manners. She had to learn judo, take lessons in shooting and gun maintenance. She was sent

42 See interview with Anne Parillaud in *Studio Magazine*, no. 61, 1992, 76–77.
43 *Ibid.*
44 *Film Français*, no. 2340, March 1988, 18. 'The gentle actress without any real character became a scandalous street-bum and then an irresistible Mata-Hari.'
45 Besson (1992) 126: 'I was proud to play his *Pygmalion* on screen.'
46 Parillaud quoted in *Studio Magazine*, no 61, 1992, 77. 'Nikita broke the little girl image that people have of women ... it broke the entire baby-doll image I had been dragging behind me.'

to acting classes to lower her voice and lose her 'titi parisienne' accent. She also went to dancing and singing classes. A whole year of strengthening the body went by before she was shown the script and told the role she was to play. It is well documented that Besson pushes Jean Reno, his friend and fetish star, into strenuous training before he plays a part in his films, but this was the first time he had demanded it of a woman actor. He had trained Parillaud up for the tough punk-junkie she would play to start with and the subsequent role she would have as the State's assassin.

The setting for this film on State terror is an imagined Paris; the architectural décor a mixture of the postmodern and the baroque. The actual sets were built in a disused cigarette factory which Besson came across in Pantin, a suburb of Paris (just beyond La Villette). The factory, now demolished, was a late 1940s' early 1950s' building – once again Besson had found a derelict space that he could recycle to his own advantage as he had done with his first film, *Le Dernier Combat*. But this time, Paris is not images-as-derelict. Like its métro in *Subway*, Paris is reconstructed, but as something less than its parts. Reinscribed as two architectural moments of excess – the one, baroque and ornate (including the stunning Train Bleu restaurant), the other, streamlined and sterile – Paris becomes familiar yet unfamiliar, an alienating, encarcerating space. And it is within this labyrinthine space that the by now familiar Bessonian theme of the search for the mother and father takes place.

Nikita tells the story of a 19-year-old punk-junkie who is given a 'second chance' in life. After being arrested in a police raid during which she shoots and kills a policeman, she is sentenced to life emprisonment. However, because she is so violent, she is dragged off to a medical centre where she is given a massive dose of a knock-out drug. She imagines she is being given a lethal dose and cries out for her mother. Later she awakens in a white cell where she is visited by a Secret Police Officer (Bob, played by Tchéky Karyo) who tells her she is officially dead – nobody, therefore, knows of her existence. He offers her the chance to 'repay' her crime by becoming an agent of the State: a State assassin. When she finally accepts the deal, she accepts to be 'reborn' again. However, her 'rebirth' is in the 'image'/under the surveillance of Bob-the-father.

She is trained up over a three-year period. But this is more than just a training. It is referred to as an education by Bob. She has to be tamed, civilised/socialised. Amande (Jeanne Moreau) helps in this process by educating her in the 'ways of women' and completing her image. As woman, Nikita is ready to fulfil her Oedipal trajectory it appears and to leave Bob-the-father's 'home'. But first she must pass Bob's final test. A first killing assignment. Even though the assignment does not go as smoothly as Bob had described it to her, she accomplishes it with flying colours (literally fleeing through a waste-chute). Her reward is her release from captivity. But of course it is also an entry into another type of captivity since she is on call for the State as their killer-agent.

Nikita, renamed Marie by the State, meets and takes home Marco (Jean-Hughes Anglade). She appears then to be making a successful transference of desire from Bob-the-father to Marco. The rest of the film is taken up with a mixture of her killing assignments and scenes of her private life with Marco – including a visit from Uncle Bob (as he has now become) who concocts a story for Marco about Nikita/Marie's past life. There are three assignments in all and her code name when working on them is Joséphine. She successfully accomplishes the first two, the second of which is to assassinate a woman in Venice when she and Marco to all intents and purposes had been sent there, by Bob, on a romantic holiday. As a 'reward' Bob gives her *carte blanche* on the third mission. In this one, she has to gain access to and film the secret files held in a proto-communist (that is, East European) embassy. She abducts the ambassador and one of her agents in her team gets set to disguise himself so that he can infiltrate the embassy. But then everything starts to go horrendously wrong and the State machinery takes over. They send in a 'cleaner', Victor (Jean Reno), who liquidates everyone except Nikita. She now cross-dresses as the ambassador and, accompanied by Victor, goes to the embassy. She gains access to the files but is spotted by the surveillance cameras and 'all hell breaks out'. Victor is killed. She escapes and disappears off the face of the earth having left the vital microfilm with Marco who now knows everything. The closing shots are of Bob and Marco seated opposite each other mourning her disappearance.

Mention was made in Chapter One that *Nikita* was shot in chronological sequence. Besson felt that it would allow for an authentic sense of Nikita's evolution from a teenage punk to a 30-something woman. It was also important to shoot in continuity, he believed, so that Anne Parillaud could let herself go completely as the punk.[47] As a result of shooting his film this way, however, it was not until he got to the end of his shooting schedule (sixteen weeks) that he realised that the ending he had scripted did not work. He quickly rescripted the end and this second version was the one adopted although he was not particularly happy with it. It is worth spelling out the earlier version and comparing it to the one finally shot – as a compromise, says Besson – because it is here that a number of problems open up around the reading of this film. In the original, first version, Marco and Nikita have been together for five years. 'Officially' she has been given three years leave to 'get a life' with Marco. However, the Secret Police come to her apartment to 'arrest' her. She makes her escape and it is Marco who dies in a shoot-out. She sets up a meeting with the Chief, and arming herself to the nines (much like Léon in his final moments) she blasts him away. She disguises herself as a journalist (she is 'méconnaissable' according to the script) and gets herself arrested for breach of the peace. Bob jumps into the car and kisses her goodbye. She makes her escape and redisguises herself as the punk of the beginning, but this time 'elle est simplement déguisée', she now has light and fight in her eyes so all resemblance to her former self is pure happenstance.[48] She holes up for two weeks in a police station as a missing person and then leaves.

This ending, on the surface of it, seems far more empowering of Nikita than the one we actually see – where she just disappears. Besson felt that, because the sentimental and emotional side of the triangular relationship between Nikita, Bob and Marco came

47 Besson (1992) 14.
48 *Ibid.*, 85.

over more strongly in the film than it had done on paper, he could not stick to the original ending which, in his words, was to be a Ramboesque firework display.[49] A third version, which he scripted for the American remake but which never got taken up, has Nikita leaving both Marco and Bob and telephoning to leave a message on Marco's answerphone which says: 'je t'aime, je vous aime.' This is the one Besson preferred and the one which he argues represented a stronger ending for Nikita.[50] He disliked the first ending by claiming that the curve of violence forced the narrative against the sentimental curve and produced an imbalance. This claim, however, says two things. First, that the love triangle/story is more important than the trajectory Nikita might have been on (and the third version does nothing to change that reading). Second, that Nikita must remain agent and, therefore, victim of the State and not subject of her own violence (as she was at the beginning of the film) or capable of agencing it in the form of violence-as-retribution (as the first end-version had her). Instead, the Nikita we are left with is one weakened by love and who must pay the price for it by disappearing off the surface of the earth. In this respect, the film is consistent with the conventions of the *film noir* it purports to emulate which has the female threat ultimately safely contained. The original ending, Ramboesque or not, would not have left any ambiguity whatsoever as to woman as agent of her own destiny. In that version, Nikita chose anonymity on her terms.

Léon (1994)

According to Parillaud and Besson, the message of *Nikita* is not one of violence but the idea that people who are full of despair and missing love are not alone.[51] This idea continues with *Léon*. In the intervening years, Besson made *Atlantis* as a way of breaking with his work of the past ten years. It is hard, however, to separate *Nikita* from *Léon* and not to see them as a continuum since in both

49 *Ibid.*, 15.
50 *Ibid.*, 92.
51 See Parillaud interview in the *Evening Standard*, 24.8.90.

narratives the central protagonists attempt to come to terms with their dysfunctionality against a background of violence which they themselves perpetrate albeit primarily as the agent for someone else. Of course violence is absolutely central to both narratives (so the above comments of Parillaud and Besson are somewhat disingenuous) and the next chapter will discuss this in detail but suffice it to say that in Léon we have a killer who is just as impressive as Nikita and whose set of suppressed needs are equal to hers bar none. It is equally difficult to perceive a clear break with *Nikita* and Besson's past film trajectory since Léon's character emanates from *Nikita* (and indeed *Le Dernier Combat*).[52] Where the two do differ, however, is in their gender, their awakening and their ending.

In a rare press exchange before *Léon* was released, Besson stated that the visible difference between the two films was one of degree: 'Tout ce que je peux vous dire sur *Léon*, c'est qu'il fera passer *Nikita* pour un film de Goretta.'[53] In other words, if we thought the degree of violence and action in *Nikita* was high, we haven't seen anything yet. Goretta, a filmmaker of the 1970s (most famous for *La Dentellière*), is an intimist, pointillist type of filmmaker more readily associated with acute observation of characters' behaviour and a gentle slow-paced rhythm to his work – hardly epithets one would ascribe to Besson's work with its fast action-shooting (*Léon* is made up of 1,540 shots, the average for a French film is around 400) and violent characterisations. In terms of violence, Léon is equipped to the nines like his spiritual father Arnold Schwarzenegger in *Terminator*, brutish like his distant cousin the beastly marauder in *Le Dernier Combat*, viciously effective like his forefather Victor in *Nikita* and a shadow of Cassavetes' avenging Gloria in the film of the same name. His

---

52 Jean Reno asked Besson to write a script for him developing the character of Victor the cleaner, Besson did and the outcome was *Léon* (see Besson (1995) 14). Once Besson had written the script, he decided he wanted to direct it. He then became unsure that Reno was the right person for the part. He wanted the best, so he checked out De Niro, Pacino, Mel Gibson before finally deciding that Reno was his number one choice (*ibid.*, 15).

53 Besson quoted in *Film Français*, no. 2543, 27.1.95.

one soft spot is his autistic behaviour which occasionally reminds us of his soul brother Dustin Hoffman in *Rain Man*.

Here is the story line. Léon, a professional but illiterate hit-man in his early forties ends up having to take under his wing a 12-year-old girl, Mathilda (Nathalie Portman), whose family has been totally annihilated by Stansfield (Gary Oldman), a corrupt police detective, over a drugs issue. Léon lives in the Little Italy district of New York and Mathilda's family are neighbours in his apartment building. Although heading up the narcotics squad, Stansfield is a dealer who enhances his salary by using the likes of Mathilda's father to sell his stuff. The deranged Stansfield, believing Mathilda's father has been cutting the cocaine for his own profit, provokes a scene so that the blood-bath that removes her entire family is disguised as a legitimate police raid. Mathilda escapes only because she had been sent on a shopping errand, to buy milk. When she returns the police are still there so she walks straight past to Léon's door. He meantime has witnessed the assault from his peep-hole. He finally lets her in and from that point forward he becomes her protector. Once the police have left, the two make their getaway and hole up in a hotel.

Until meeting Mathilda, Léon is an automaton – professionally primed to kill at the behest of his boss with the one exception that he will kill neither women nor children. He is apparently without feeling, and is regressively turned back within himself. Indeed, Besson describes him as a 12-year-old within a 40-year-old body. And there are many signs pointing to his retreat into infantilism. He has no attachments except to his one green plant that he tends to with great solicitude. He is a contract killer and yet he drinks milk (not whiskey!), a first degree of infantilisation. He banks his money with his Mafia contract boss Tony (Danny Aïello), the local Italian restaurateur. Léon cannot read or write, a second degree of infantilisation. He is simple-minded, naïve and asexual, a third degree of infantilisation. He lacks language, is seemingly autisitic – a condition normally associated with childhood, a fourth degree of infantilisation. His dress code (non-existent in fact) – a cross between Chaplin and Jacques Tati – is the absolute reverse of what one would expect of a professional killer: his trousers are too short, his coat too big.[54] Within his 40-year-old body he carries a 12-year-old boy, but his clothes reveal an exteriorisation of the child within – a fifth and last degree of infantilisation. Conversely, the streetwise Mathilda is a 12-year-old girl on the brink of adolescence and sexual awareness and knowledgeable beyond her years. As soon as she discovers that Léon is a contract killer, she determines to acquire his skills and demands that he teach her so that she can avenge the murder of her little brother (the only one in her selfish and brutish family who was loving and whom she loved).

As Léon trains Mathilda up to hit-woman standard so their relationship develops from a proto father–daughter one to that of chaste lovers. Léon's asexuality ensures the innocence of this love rather than Mathilda's burgeoning sexuality, it has to be said (more on this later). Mathilda, in the meantime, teaches Léon to read. She also discovers that Stansfield works at the Department of Justice (the DEA office) and decides to connive her way in (delivering fast food) and kill him. The plan backfires and Stansfield traps her in the men's room. She is taken upstairs for questioning. Léon comes to her rescue having *read* a note she left him telling him of her whereabouts. Stansfield, enraged, is determined to dragnet them and wipe them out. He finds out where they are staying (by bullying Tony, Léon's Mafia contract boss, a weak and ambiguous character at best) and sets off with enough Special Police to storm a fortress. He takes Mathilda hostage (she has again gone shopping for food). Léon manages to shoot his way out of the first assault and get Mathilda back. In the second assault, he opens up a heating-vent and propels Mathilda down the shaft to safety (shades of Nikita), but not before they make a mutual declaration of love. By now Léon is seriously wounded. Nonetheless, he still has the strength to trap a Secret Policeman in the room, kill him, don his outfit (including a

---

54 Reno speaks of his costume as enabling him to inhabit his dual role as violent killer and tender emotional human being. The coat was stiff and uncomfortable, making him stand rigid (much like a child ill at ease with its new clothes that are slightly on the large side and definitely practical), whereas the boots were no-nonsense 'shit-kickers' (Reno, in Besson (1995) 106).

balaclava helmet) and make his escape – but only to the foyer of the hotel. Stansfield spots him and shoots him. As he lies dying he hands Stansfield the pin to a grenade, declaring 'this is for Mathilda', and blows up his body and kills the evil Stansfield in the process. Mathilda makes her escape and returns to the boarding school she had abandoned earlier on and relates her fantastic story to explain her absenteeism. The last shot is of her planting Léon's much-loved green plant in the school grounds.

Léon raises a number of problematic issues around sexuality and regression and I want to dwell just briefly on them before concluding this chapter (Chapter Four looks at this question again within the larger context of the father–mother narrative that acts as a subtext to all Besson's films). Part of this discussion brings me back to the similarities between this film and *Nikita*. *Léon* is in many ways the mirror image of *Nikita*. Although gender-wise they are of opposite sexes and Léon goes out with the Ramboesque ending denied Nikita, and although Léon's awakening to his affective side comes about as a result of his encounter with a child whereas Nikita's develops from her relationship with an adult, nonetheless the infantilisation of the two protagonists is quite similar as is their trajectory through violence to an understanding of love. In this regard, there are clear parallels between Léon's characterisation and Nikita's. Within this cold killer there resides a sensitive being who is himself a victim (of lack of love, hence the milk). Finally, it is hard not to see Mathilda as the child-woman version of the woman-child Nikita – as a regression therefore to a former type.

In *Nikita*, the relationship that causes primary concern is the one between Bob and Nikita, because one reading would be that she is punished for it. However, it has none of the resonances of *Léon* where there is something profoundly worrying about the love relationship between Mathilda and Léon that switches from a father–daughter one to a quasi-incestuous one. Indeed, these resonances were cause for concern at the time of the film's release, the context of which is as follows. *Léon* was Besson's first full foray into international film production. The film was co-produced by Gaumont and Les Films du Dauphin on the French side, Columbia[55] on the American and JVC on the Japanese. It cost $16 million to produce (approximately 80 million francs) and was marketed in the USA as an American film made by the director of *La Femme Nikita*. It was renamed *The Professional* to give it that American-made movie cachet of authenticity. In exchange for selling the American distribution rights of the film to Columbia, Besson retained the right to the final cut (unheard of in Hollywood). Columbia in return guaranteed a full release in the USA in 1,200 theatres (*Nikita* was released in only 100). However, as an American product, the film had to go through screen tests. One scene in particular met with general opprobrium and not a little dash of political correctness. Once Léon has rescued Mathilda from the DEA office, they return to their hotel and Mathilda puts on a pretty dress given her by Léon. She then declares her love for him and tells him she wants him to be her first lover. Léon, uncomprehending and panicking, refuses. Besson perceived it as a tender moving moment, the American test audience hated it, seeing it as perverse and paedophiliac. Besson was furious at the reaction. His film was about love, pure love. Not about sex, which is all the Americans could see.[56] To mollify the American producers, but more to ensure that the film would get full general release, Besson agreed to cut the 'offending' scene. At the next screening test the ratings went up from 19 per cent to 31 per cent – still not blanket approval but enough to merit full release.[57]

When released, American critics still panned it for its quasi-child pornography.[58] But, as it gained in popularity amongst American audiences, some changed their tune. Besson felt that by cutting the 'offending' scene he ruined the meaning of the later declaration of mutual love in the heating-duct before they separate

55 Although we must recall that Columbia is currently owned by the Japanese company Sony.

56 Besson (1995) 45.

57 Besson re-released the film in France in 1996 as a full director's cut, reinserting this 'offending' scene and editing in one or two others developing the relationship between Mathilda and Léon – lengthening the film by twenty-five minutes.

58 See the review in *Films in Review*, vol. 46, no. 1/2, 1995, 55–56.

which now came over as far too strong. Possibly, however, the *mise-en-scène* did not help lighten the meaning. In this, their last goodbye, she is about to drop down the hole he has opened up for her in the heating-duct! As with Nikita's disappearance down a rubbish-chute it is not hard to read this scene as a containment and displacement of female sexuality. Furthermore, there are earlier moments when this platonic relationship of love borders on the incestuous and uneasy, even to the European eye.[59] Moments such as Mathilda's bold fantasy uttered to the hotel porter that she and Léon are not father and daughter (as they had pretended to be when registering) but lovers; and again when she plays her dressing-up game in which she impersonates, in turn, *the* iconic sex-goddesses of America, Madonna and Marilyn Monroe (to the complete mystification of Léon it must be said). Of course, it could be countered that these are games, and that as such they constitute part of the child's development, including sexual development. And if we accept that this part of the narrative at least is told from Mathilda's point of view, then the film does represent the child-to-adolescent's subjectivity and her fantasy enactments can be read as driven by a desire to parody adult behaviour – but not necessarily to be part of it.

Besson, in interview after interview, has expressed his dismay at the thought that his film has any sexual overtones. 'I was interested in talking about pure love. Society today confuses love and sex. On a street poster, the girl is still beautiful and naked, even if it is an ad for chocolate. The more society develops, the more we act like beasts. That is why I chose to talk about two twelve-year-olds, even though one is actually 40.'[60] If anything, Besson is arguing that this is a regressive and, therefore, innocent love. And there is strong enough evidence that this film, in its denial of adulthood and sexuality, bears some striking parallels not just with *Nikita* but also with *Subway* and *Le Grand Bleu*. So it is not a new theme. However, this theme of regression is double-edged, not least because the camerawork goes counter to a singular reading. The accusation is not that there is a false *naïveté*

59 See the review in *Sight and Sound*, vol. 5, no. 2, 1995, 47–48.
60 Interview with Besson in the *Guardian*, 2.2.95.

about Besson's declarations, but that the very theme of regression, double-edged as it is, has much to say about the perceived and actual position of youth in contemporary society. It is also, when it comes to female characterisation, equally revealing of an unchanging misogyny in French cinema that dates back at least to the 1930s if not indeed to its beginnings.

Conclusion

Stylisation and excess are hallmarks of Besson's work. Characters are larger than life, décors are in excess of their referent in their hyper-realism. And yet both are less than the signs to which they refer. Besson's characters lack psychological depth and his sets reduce the city to a topography of the ugly or the grandiose, the derelict or the plutocratic. The sumptuous and the ornate cohabit with the violent and the vulgar. Excess and violence – this is the terrestrial world in which Besson's characters are held captive, the world we like to repress and believe does not exist. In this respect, the décor *is* the mirror to the characterisation. Nobody fits into this décor (not even the dolphin who has to be rescued from the dolphinarium in *Le Grand Bleu*). Hence the constant desire to escape at any price. Hence also the labyrinthine nature of the world that incarcerates Léon, Nikita, Fred. Small wonder we see so little representation of the cityscape. To the lack of visible city space corresponds the lack of actual social equilibrium. This is the world of the lost generation where terrestrial mothers and fathers are absent, where the policing effects of technology and surveillance maintain a culture of 'othering', and where self-fulfilment ultimately means embracing disappearance or an early death.

Besson's use of excess is also extremely playful. He mixes violence with humour (long before Tarantino saw it as a good idea), primitive cinema with the *bande dessinée*. Food is very much back on the menu in Besson's films and is never neutral in its function. Genres are hybridised to the point where they are reduced to a degree zero, and sometimes this hybridisation fails (as with *Le Grand Bleu*). His playfulness is as much an attraction as is his more serious representation of the world. And it is here that Besson is inherently a populist filmmaker because he appeals to the cultural competences and dispositions of consumers of popular culture – the elite or cinephilic can either take it or leave it as far as he is concerned.

This is arguably a major reason for the more intellectual film journals' rejection of his work. And the sociologist Pierre Bourdieu's analysis of taste is helpful in this context.[61] According to Bourdieu, there are three categories of taste which are strongly linked to class formation in terms of economic and cultural capital. These categories of taste are: legitimate (or élite), middlebrow, popular. According to Bourdieu, these categories of taste explain how class distinctions are produced. Because different sections of society have different competences and dispositions they will consume cultural forms in different ways. What Bourdieu means by cultural capital is that just as differences in classes are marked by the access they have to economic capital, so too they are marked by their differing access to culture. Thus the working classes do not have the same access to an Italian Renaissance painting as do the wealthy classes. Even if they could make their way to Italy, the way that the working classes would read the painting would differ from the reading the rich would impose on the same painting. And the reason for this would be because their cultural capital (their distinct knowledges that they bring to the painting) would be different. Bourdieu argues that class difference is the product of differential access to cultural capital. The cultural capital possessed by social groups is what determines their competences and dispositions. Cultural competences refer to the skills and knowledge which enable us to make sense of certain types of cultural material but not necessarily others (thus a certain class can understand a piece of music that may not be understood by another – a piece of Ligetti music say, or a rap-song). Cultural dispositions refer to the effect of the differential

61 See Pierre Bourdieu (1984) *Distinction: A Social Critique of the Judgement of Taste*, London, Routledge; and for a helpful introduction to questions of popular culture and film, see Joanne Hollows and Mark Jancovich (eds) (1995) *Approaches to Popular Film*, Manchester, Manchester University Press.

distribution of capital upon our consumption practices, that is, how we choose to consume what culture is available to us. Thus, in relation to film, certain groups will have the cultural competence/baggage to understand and appreciate a futurist sci-fi film (such as *Blade Runner*), others a heritage film (such as *Sense and Sensibility*), others still a European art film (such as Kieslowski's trilogy, *Bleu, Blanc, Rouge*). Some groups may well be able to make sense of all three types of film which could be described as popular, middlebrow and elite. However, they may well prefer to see one type of film over the others because of their cultural disposition. Besson's work is popular culture and, at present, pulls greatly on youth-knowledge. His films address the cultural capital of a social group that is by and large under 35 years of age.

The other useful point to make in relation to Besson's work and its rejection by intellectual film journals (particularly French ones) again comes from Bourdieu. The ability to recognise legitimate/élite culture depends on the possession of a cultural capital or aesthetic that, in turn, is based upon a rejection of the popular aesthetic (or taste) – that is, you cannot have a concept of high art without having also a concept of low art (which you then reject as lacking). Legitimate culture then depends on a rejection of popular culture. However, what is less well understood is that popular taste is based upon a refusal of that refusal. It is not so much the case that certain social groups are unable to appreciate legitimate culture as it is that they reject what appreciating such culture entails. 'Legitimate' culture depends on distance to be appreciated, popular culture on participation. By distance what is meant is that legitimate culture rarefies the object by aestheticising it so that its form has greater value over its function. For example, we go to an art museum to look at a painting. We go to look at its form. Popular culture reverses that perception or, better still, dissolves it. Punk subculture is a good example of this, bringing form and function together as a popular cultural artefact. But we could also quote the Mod culture of the 1960s and its love of Italian scooters, paradoxically the acme of aesthetic design but available to the many. Legitimate art excludes by not responding to a demand for participation, we go to look at not to use the art object. It rejects popular culture as mass-produced and standardised.

In the meantime, popular culture believes in the principle of access and participation and welcomes technology's ability to multiply rather than rarefy pleasure. In this context then Besson's films encourage participation. He entices spectators to come and see his films through his appropriation of technology (scope and dolby sound) and the representation of the world he offers. As such, his films challenge the culturally empowered and their desire to keep the distinction between high and low art alive – indeed, he challenges their motivation in rejecting his form of popular culture. This does not mean to say, however, that there are no problems with Besson's cultural artefacts, any more than there are none with other cultural artefacts (high or low). His films disturb as much as they please and it is this that we are going to examine, amongst other things, in the next two chapters.

1 The hero (Pierre Jolivet) and his costume made of recycled waste (*Le Dernier Combat*, 1983)

2 The gang leader (Fritz Wepper) and his necklace of fingers (*Le Dernier Combat*, 1983)

3 Isabelle Adjani as Héléna (*Subway*, 1985)

4 Fred (Christophe Lambert) enters the métro's familiar unfamiliarity (*Subway*, 1985)

5 Male rivalry or brotherly love? Enzo (Jean Reno) and Jacques (Jean-Marc Barr) exchange looks (*Le Grand Bleu*, 1988)

6 The transgressive male, Enzo (Jean Reno), as subject and object of his death (*Le Grand Bleu*, 1988)

7 Jacques's (Jean-Marc Barr) true desire; the sea-mother-lover (*Le Grand Bleu*, 1988)

8 Anne Parillaud as the punk Nikita and director Luc Besson (*Nikita*, 1990)

9 Bob-the-father (Tchéky Karyo) in probing mood (*Nikita*, 1990)

10 Nikita (Anne Parillaud) dressed to kill on her first assignment (*Nikita*, 1990)

11 Léon (Jean Reno) the robotic hit-man (*Léon*, 1994)

12 Mathilda (Nathalie Portman) the child-woman (*Léon*, 1994)

3

Violence as performance

All Besson's films have violence at the core of the narrative. But this is not just a case of 'designer-violence' although of course that is there too (to compete with American products of the same ilk). More importantly, violence is inscribed on to, written on the body. The body becomes the site of violence. More significantly still, violence is represented not just through any body but, in a very primary sense, through that of the main protagonist. In other words, the site of representation for violence is the star text. The star text, amongst other things, functions as reflectors of the time and as signs that reflect into society. Stars embody our aspirations as much as they embody cultural and social values (we all 'wannabe' some star or another). Stars reach us, primarily, through their bodies – we watch their appearance and their performance. Besson's stars, viewed in this light, become inter-esting 'texts' to read. His stars embody/impersonate the tension that melds violence with fragility (be it Jean Reno, Christophe Lambert, or Anne Parillaud). And, as we can see, in his films it is a tension which is not restricted to a particular gender. According to society, says Besson, women are not supposed to feel violent but that is mere conditioning, they do feel violent, it is just that they are simply not supposed to express it. At the end of a Besson film, the star text disappears (either literally or through death). So the question becomes, what is Besson telling us through his stars' embodying/embodiment of violence? Hence the title of this chapter which will seek to answer this question.

In Besson's films technology functions as an extension of this violence and it is a two-way system of surveillance and counter-surveillance that often involves death. Cameras and weaponry watch and kill. Surveillance and death come together in the form of high-powered long-distance rifles with telescopic lenses which proliferate in Besson's films. Even the superficially non-violent *Le Grand Bleu* abounds with camera technology. These camera-eyes function as instruments of investigation and surveillance. The star text uses them to observe and destroy, but they are also used to observe the star text and destroy her/him. Technology, the body and death are closely interlinked concepts in Besson narratives and a central core component to their imaging is violence.

In order to understand the significance of this presence of technology in Besson's work, we need to examine how this technology of surveillance and death has come into being in the first place. We then need to understand how and why systems of technology are bound to the body in the form of projections of repressed fears. Then we can look at Besson's films and investigate this interface between technology and the body and examine the environments in which these violent interactions *between* the body and technology, as well as *within* the body, are played out. Performance, display and voyeurism are key ways of approaching these issues, as is a discussion of the socio-political questions Besson addresses in his films. Conformity and control are the social norms that are institutionally sanctioned and yet they represent as much a form of violence as any other. Besson's protagonists – whilst they may embody forms of violence – reject, fail or are unwilling to adapt to contemporary society, to its own particular form of violence. And they express that refusal or failure through violence to their self. There is no 'happy ending' *à l'américaine*.

The first part of this chapter examines questions of violence, particularly in relation to the so-called youth in crisis, and discusses these issues within the context of surveillance and technology. The second part of this chapter will look at Besson's films as the *mise-en-scène* of the double cult of technology and commodified capitalism within the context of technology and the body.

Youth in crisis – surveillance – technology – death

I have deliberately not fully hyphenated these key words. However, they are signifiers of the times of the 1980s and 1990s and are concepts that are readily embodied or represented in Besson's films – particularly in *Le Dernier Combat, Nikita,* and *Léon.* I shall therefore be focusing on these three films, but reference will also be made to *Subway* and *Le Grand Bleu.* I want to make it clear that these four concepts are not to be seen as a causal chain, but rather as a cluster of meanings. Nor are they signs, but concepts referring to a perceived reality – which is why I have chosen the term 'signifier': the signified may or may not be 'true', the signifiers refer, then, to a perceived 'truth'. The following outline, indeed mapping, of these concepts should serve to make this clear and I will illustrate them by referring to Besson's work.

My first line of argument is that, progressively over the 1980s and 1990s, youth has increasingly come under public surveillance as the family has lost its 'rightful' claim to surveillance as supervisor and reproducer of the social order. This has, in turn, led to a form of 'moral panic' about 'youth in crisis' – there is of course a hidden agenda to this which I will come to in a minute. But this shift from private (parental supervision) to public surveillance leads to my second line of argument which is that surveillance is above all technology-led these days and that youth – in that it is surveilled – is imaged and imagined as spectacle and therefore cannot help displaying itself. This in turn raises questions around voyeurism and fetishism in relation to youth. My last line of argument addresses three related issues. First, that technology (primarily surveillance technology) functions as a containment and displacement of man's anxiety around sexuality (his sexuality but also that of the female) and as such is a sign of regression, not progression; second, that technology reproduces power relations; and third, that technology in its automatism functions as a ready sign for death.[1]

1 I have used several sources to help map out these arguments and am particularly indebted to the following authors: Charles R. Acland (1995) *Youth, Murder, Spectacle,* Boulder, San Francisco, Oxford, Westview Press; Dick Hebdige (1988)

Youth in crisis – surveillance – technology

Mention was made at the beginning of the previous chapter that the youth class in France is one that has faced the disempowering effect of mass unemployment and experienced a concomitant sense of disfranchisement since the early 1980s. This so-called *génération Mitterrand* is in fact one that has become labelled a generation in crisis (20 per cent of the unemployed class is under 25 years of age). Theirs is a climate of little hope for the future; a 'no-hopism' which displays itself, according to police and sociologists' reports, through dysfunctional behaviour in the form of drug abuse, violent crime and sexual promiscuity.[2] And yet, as an economic class, the youth class is largely a disempowered one – they are outside the social order of things precisely because they do not have work. A great majority of young people do not have the capital power to participate in the culture of consumption that surrounds them – not, that is, unless they find ways of generating capital for themselves: and this usually means prostitution, drug-dealing, theft. So this dysfunctional behaviour is a self-fulfilling prophecy. Further, we are told that this generation in crisis retreats into fantasy and then confuses fantasy with reality – thus video-games (a.k.a *Dungeon and Dragons*) and violent films become reflections of a reality they will mimic. At the same time reports tell us that one frightening aspect of youth violence is its meaninglessness.[3] Meaningless to whom? In a society where consumption is all, what else can a class that cannot engage in the economic activity of that society do but register its anger or antagonism towards an environment that excludes them? Graffiti, skate-boarding in shopping malls, pick-pocketing, pan-handling, mugging, looting – these are all perceived forms of youth aggression, gratuitous acts of violence – but they are gratuitous, meaningless only because they challenge the accepted definitions

Hiding in the Light, London and New York, Routledge; John Orr (1993) *Cinema and Modernity*, Cambridge, Polity Press; Jean Baudrillard (1996) *The System of Objects* (trans. James Benedict), London and New York, Verso.

2 A new unholy trinity to replace that of the 1960s: sex, drugs and rock 'n' roll.

3 For more detail, see Acland (1995) 3–7.

of social space, they strike at the very heart of what everyone else understands by the social space (as exemplified by the city). In other words, this is a process whereby youth in crisis can be reconstructed as youth gone wild.[4] This is youth culture at its most wanton. And one that must be contained. It is not difficult to see this as a process of demonising that spreads over to other youth cultural forms by association (music, dress-code, street performers, etc.).

The 1960s' generation struggled to free itself of parental supervision and, thanks largely to its significant size (the so-called baby-boomers), it was successful in its struggle. However, youth is a period when the social order of things (and this includes consumption practices, of course) are learned and so it is a 'natural' time of supervision, surveillance.[5] If that supervision is no longer in the hands of the private domesticated sphere then it 'logically' will resurface in the public one. The more youth is perceived to have 'gone wild', the more the public at large will defer – out of a sense of panic, moral panic in effect, but which is called common sense – to an increase in systems of surveillance. Thus we witness the abundance of cameras, CCTVs (close-circuit TV cameras), an increase in the policing of petty crime and in the number of store detectives.[6] It is noteworthy that most of these surveillance systems prevail in areas of commodified capitalism (shops, shopping centres, banks, etc.) as well as along the institutionalised routes to these areas (métro, bus), or within the access stations to them (railway stations and airports, for example).

Youth in crisis as a concept assumes that there is a social order from which it deviates. In other words, there is a process of 'othering', pointing to the youth class as 'other', as a threat to the stability of the social order. And the question remains what purpose does this structuring of otherness serve. As Acland rightly says, 'youth as constructed in the 1980s is a site at which the struggles between order and crisis take place'.[7] So the discourses

4 *Ibid.*, 10–13.

5 *Ibid.*, 25.

6 We note that now even schools imitate the judiciary system in their attempts to police youth disarray through their own internal courts (to deal with bullies, thieves, etc.).

7 Acland (1995) 13.

and representations of youth delinquency are ultimately a projection of society's anxiety around the reproduction of the social order.
Those 'within' the said social order of things speak of a youth in
crisis as a way of expressing their fear that the social order of
things is unstable and in crisis. Thus, the issue is one of displacement and containment. By displacing the concept of crisis on to
youth, the threat of a crisis to hegemony is contained. It is placed
outside the social order of things – on to youth – that is, on to an
age class that is in no position truly to threaten that social order of
things. Finally, then, and paradoxically, the concept of the 'other'
is important to social stability.[8]

Before pursuing the next line of argument (youth as spectacle),
it would be useful to tie some of these ideas into general points
that we can make about Besson's films. In Jean-Luc Godard's film
A bout de souffle (1959), a young woman asks Michel Poiccard
(played by Jean-Paul Belmondo) if he has anything against youth
('vous n'avez rien contre la jeunesse' she asks). He replies that he
does and that he prefers old people ('si, je préfère les vieux').
Besson's films unmask that section of society that dislikes youth,
those defenders of commodity capitalism who cannot accommodate the 'other', who see youth as the enemy within. Besson's
protagonists break boundaries (*Nikita*), set up alternative systems
to the system of capitalism (as in *Subway*). Meantime, the older
generation, the representatives of social order, are constantly seeking – through surveillance – to remove them, or contain and
detain them. What is not wanted is a new social order of things,
but a recycling and reproduction of what was there before.
Besson's characters stand out by their regressive nature, their
refusal to enter the social order and reproduce, and finally by their
desire to go back *beyond* the womb or to disappear. The meta-
phoric presence of the uterus (or the route to it) in Besson's films
as a wasteland (*Le Dernier Combat* and *Subway*), as a rubbish-chute

8 We are perhaps more used to other forms of 'othering' based on race and gender
   difference for example, or indeed national differences. In western society, if we
   are white and middle-class and male we are more inclined to feel safe than a
   black male or female because we are assured our place in the social order of
   things through our sameness.

(*Nikita*), or a heat-duct (*Léon*), or indeed as death (*Le Grand Bleu*) makes abundantly clear the message of resistance to the hegemonic concept of the family as a stable unit and reproducer of the social order.

Youth as crisis – surveillance – technology – spectacle

Since the 1950s (certainly the 1960s) there has been a visibilisation of youth. What started out as a rhetoric of concern, fear for youth, has progressively evolved into one of moral panic, fear of youth.[9] As Dick Hebdige says, 'youth is only present when its presence is a problem'.[10] And its visibility, as Acland argues,[11] comes down to three categories – all of which are part of the rhetoric of concern and which represent youth as an object for the critical gaze, as a cultural concern, and as a social category.[12] This rhetoric, these discourses surrounding youth are both a verbalisation and visibilisation of relations of power: youth is visualised as deviant, as a spectacle of otherness. Youth is not part of the centre: for a start, it has not yet arrived there, economically speaking. But, because it is seen to occupy a social site on the outside (the periphery), it occupies a site that contradicts that of the centre and often challenges the safe borders of dominant ideology. When it breaks bounds, it issues 'rhetorical challenges [of its own] to the law'.[13] Such then are the discourses emanating from this rhetoric of concern. However, part of the 'problem' of youth is of course that it contains within its own representation of itself a 'livisibility' (a visible rhetoric) that 'we', inside the social order, cannot read.[14] We fear its unreadability and construct its unreadability as fearsome. What we are talking about here is a fetishisation of youth, a spectacularisation of youth-as-violence

9 See Acland (1995) 25 and 143.
10 Hebdige (1988) 17.
11 Acland (1995) 25.
12 *Ibid.*
13 Hebdige (1988) 18.
14 I am indebted to my friend and colleague Jean-François Diana of the University of Metz for this very precise and playful term *livisibilité*: a merging of 'lisibilité' and 'visibilité' giving a meaning of visually readable.

(breaking bounds) which says more about our fears of the very real changing boundaries of class, gender and race that 'surround' us than it does about the youth class as a fundamental threat to the social order of things. Why else do we imagine youth as a single social category, as a unity, when they are as diverse as any other age group? Displacement and containment is once again at work.

Our desire to construct youth as crisis and to look at it reveals a profound ambivalence towards that generation. A mistrust that echoes the earlier representation of women in the American *film noir* of the late 1940s. Discourses around youth reveal a paranoia at its transgressiveness and yet a fascination and a desire to investigate it (youth, that is). In much the same way as the female in the *film noir* was fetishised and made into an object of speculation but who nonetheless by the end of the film (having been thoroughly looked at) would be punished for her trans-gressiveness, so too youth is commodified as transgressive. Youth is punished for its transgressiveness, but also fetishised as revered object – as object that cannot be read, understood, and therefore must be contained as fetish. Revered also, because, in the final analysis, youth is the 'outside' (the 'other') that must (is to) become 'inside' (the upholder of the social order of things). After all, youth is our necessary future, we 'pin our hopes' on them – but this hope is deeply ambivalent. There is a tension between the desire to control youth as other and the despair at *our* (imagined and imaged) inability to do so. Acland makes the point that many youth films of the 1980s and 1990s do not represent the youth's point of view at all although they may well pretend to in that they 'caution adults about youth'.[15] Rather, they systematically resecure the narrative into the fully socialised adult gaze. Youth is constructed as the object to be looked at. Youth movies become the *mise-en-scène* of 'the enticing nature of the spectacle of wasted youth, of youth gone wild'.[16]

In Chapter Two I mentioned that one of the criticisms levelled at Besson was that he plays guru to the youth audience. Some

15 Acland (1995) 116.
16 Acland (1995) 118. We could add that this was a trope of a fair number of 1950s' Hollywood films starring Marlon Brando, James Dean and Montgomery Clift.

critics even accuse him of practising a racism of exclusion in relation to the older generation. It would seem rather that a central motivation of Besson's films is to represent youth's point of view but not in a simplistic way. Besson's films hold the adult gaze up for inspection and, in so doing, they serve to expose, as it were, the politics of youth-as-spectacle and the system of labelling them as outsiders. In fact, his films expose the effects of the fully socialised adult gaze and turn it around on itself. This is surely a dominant theme of *Nikita*, but one that is present already in *Subway* in that the young 'deviants' underground are subject to the constant scrutiny of the métro police (the surveillance and pursuit of the roller-skater exemplifies this) – the spectator is privy to the essentialising gaze of the adult.

The politics of youth are then to do with the politics of spectacle.[17] The dominant discourses on youth suggest that they are anomic types, that it is a case of them choosing to stay outside of society rather than society excluding them – 'they' do not and have chosen not to fit in with the prevailing norms. But this, as we have suggested, is to provide an easy reason for so-called youth violence and serves to justify the culture of surveillance-technology in which they are made to live. Surveillance is not a new phenomenon, of course. And in the past as in the present it is its benign properties and intentions that have been signalled as of uppermost importance and utility. Michel Foucault, in his study of the society of surveillance, recalls the humanist intention behind Jeremy Bentham's Panopticon: a circular architectural structure where cells are arranged around a central viewing tower ensuring permanent visibility (the prisoners watch themselves being watched). Bentham had intended this imagined system of prison surveillance (where all watch all) as a substitute for the brutality of cell imprisonment and an alternative to the cruel treatment handed out to prisoners.[18] The panopticon principle was based in the belief that, if everyone watches everyone else, then transgressive behaviour on any one's part becomes impossible

17 Acland (1995) 20.
18 See Michel Foucault (1977) *Discipline and Punish: The Birth of the Prison* (trans. A. M. Sheridan-Smith), Harmondsworth, Penguin.

because it will be seen. What Bentham was proposing was a 'benign' form of visual rather than corporeal censorship. But of course once the principle of total surveillance has been posited it is self-evident that, once implemented, the final outcome will be far from benign and that it will become an instrument of social control and repression. By its very nature as a cheap and efficacious system of permanent and total visibility it ensures that its uses will not be limited to prisons, but that it will spread out into other social spheres.

Indeed, as an example of this shift from benign purpose to repressive function we could look at what happened to the still camera, at first a new technological instrument for 'catching life'. It was not enough to catch one's own life, other, philanthropic uses were soon found for it. It was taken out into the streets, down into mines, over to African and Indian continents, all in the name of benign, ethnographic observation. Thus, to return to our subject of inquiry, once this technology for mass observation became accessible, youth (amongst other groups) soon became an object for scrutiny.[19] Hebdige makes the point that surveillance of youth can be traced back to the nineteenth century and the mass observation of street life that was commodified as a philanthropic investigation of hardship.[20] This investigation of youth took the form of documentation through photography and written reports. The progression from documentary reportage to intervention is, as Hebdige says, an evident one.[21] Documentation functions to facilitate the administration of the urban setting but this cannot mask the power relationships inscribed into documentary practice in which the documenter is a 'concerned voyeuristic subject' and the documented are the 'object of our pity, fear and fascination'.[22]

We even offer these objects of our pity (and fear) the chance of redemption – saving them from themselves. Hebdige points to

19 Miners, including women miners in the North of England, were objects for documentary scrutiny; African men and women in the colonies, their tribal nudity/otherness was just one other.

20 Hebdige (1988) 20–21.

21 *Ibid.*

22 Hebdige (1988) 22.

the Dr Barnardo Homes as one example. Youth training schemes are a more contemporary one. There were several put in place in France during the 1980s, of which the TUC (*travaux d'utilité communautaire*) was one. A form of cheap and unskilled community labour it was pitifully paid and much derided by France's youth class. Their systematic rejection of the State's attempt to put them to work (no matter how meaningless the task) was for a while a favoured television news item. Of a 'random' ten youths interviewed, typically, all but one would declare that the TUC fulfilled no purpose whatsoever. Their overriding refusal to see any value to the TUC was mediated as deviant: this was the ungrateful, lazy youth-class which cannot see that the State is doing its level best in a time of economic crisis. This entirely misses the point that youth resents being 'conscripted' into and commodified as cheap labour. This cheapening of the value of youth is a profoundly undemocratic practice which unsurprisingly breeds a feeling of entrenched disenchantment amongst young people. Eric Rochant's film *Un monde sans pitié* (1990) exemplifies this perfectly: the central protagonist cannot be bothered to find work since there is no work to be found – he is educated, could go to university but sees no point. Nikita's trajectory, in Besson's film of that name, can partly be read in this light. The redemption she is offered for coming off drugs and off the street is to become a lackey of the State, to rechannel her violence at the service of the State. In other words, she is obliged to recycle her murdering skills within the legitimate arena of the State – more specifically within the arena of France's Secret Service, surely *the* institutional centre of the centre (within the social order, the law), *the* eye of the society of surveillance. Viewed in this light, her rejection, at the end of the film, of her ascribed role as State-assassin, her refusal to participate any further can be read as a form of resistance.

Of course, as we suggested in the last chapter, Nikita's resistance is double-edged since the price to pay is disappearance – 'not being'. Since youth marks by its presence, it is probably safe to say that absence is a place/space to which society would like to confine it. And it is for this reason that youth – as a form of resistance to this desire to invisibilise – chooses to 'hide in the light' (to recoin Hebdige's phrase). Hebdige's suggestion that hiding in the light is a form of resistance shows how it is difficult, ultimately, to read positively Nikita's strategy for survival (if indeed she is allowed to survive). Hebdige's first point is that youth culture as 'a sign-system centres on the body – on appearance, posture, dress'.[23] His argument is that as a disempowered class, the one site where youth can exert its power is through their own bodies: that much they own. Thus, 'the body can be decorated' or, conversely, 'it can be cut up to look like a piece of meat'.[24] Self-mutilation, punk hairstyles and dress-codes are markers, not so much of difference, but of the 'disavowal of the will to queue for work'.[25] Hebdige's second point concerns the way in which that body is viewed. Since it knows it is being watched, 'it translates the fact of being under scrutiny into the pleasure of being watched'.[26] This is hiding in the light. It is a double-edged response. On the one hand it is 'a declaration of independence, of otherness' and a 'refusal of anonymity and subordinate status'. On the other it is 'a confirmation of the fact of powerlessness, a celebration of impotence'.[27] Knowing that they are to be seen, youth displays the body-as-visible, yet it refuses to be 'livisible' (we cannot read or make sense of the body we see).

At the beginning of *Nikita*, Nikita is not livisible. Throughout her training period, she stands out through her embodied otherness: in her appearance, posture and dress. She repeatedly attempts to assert herself and refuse a subordinate status. Her graffitied cell-walls are an extension of her 'decorated body' at the same time as they are an acknowledgement of her impotence and powerlessness against the State that surveilles her. During this whole period she turns her 'to-be-looked-at-ness' into an aggressive act – refusing the conventional iconography of the woman as object of the gaze. However, her rhetorical challenges to the law are short-lived and she is finally tamed into woman – this is the

23 Hebdige (1988) 31.
24 *Ibid.*, 31–32.
25 *Ibid.*, 32.
26 *Ibid.*, 35.
27 *Ibid.*

only way she is allowed to 'move forward', that is, to live. She has to come inside from the outside, enter the 'social order of things' – otherwise she must accept death. As Bob says, once she has been brought (kicking and screaming) inside, she is now 'un élément du centre'. From that moment on she is the programmable object that can be sent on assignments. All agency and disavowal have gone. From now on, she is no longer just visible to the State, she is also livisible in the surveillance eye of the State. The former subversion of the eye of the camera is at an end: no more hiding in the light. Instead, she enters a different relationship of ambivalence with the eye of the camera. As State-assassin, it is she who looks down the telescopic lens of her weapon to hit her target. She becomes the eye of the camera – the camera that observes then kills. However, her eye is trained and dictated to by the voice of the State (telling her who to kill). We even get a counter-shot of Nikita's eye viewed down the telescopic lens just to make the point. She is not, therefore, the 'I' of the camera, but object. She is not agent of her viewing in other words. At this stage she is exposed to the light, no longer hiding in it. Essentially naked in the light, she is still on display as before, but this time her powerlessness is greater because it is minus the resistance. Her body is no longer the site of disavowal (it is working for the State). Power, in the form of violence is now inscribed *on to* it – not *in* it as had been the case before when she owned her body, when it acted as her cultural sign-system of refusal and insubordination. The next stage in her trajectory is the end of everything. Nikita has to 'de-visibilise' herself. She is no longer *in* the eye of the camera, nor indeed the eye *of* the camera framing the target. The light has completely gone out. The spectacle is over. The early moment of narcissism, however bleak, is but a distant memory.

Youth – surveillance – technology – sexuality – death

Surveillance, as described in the previous section, suggests that something more complex is at work than a single-system of looks. Indeed, the relay of looks is a closed circuit between, on the one hand, the camera that looks and, on the other, the object's awareness of the camera's scrutiny. That awareness can manifest itself through a deliberate display of the body as site/sight of resistance. Or the body can respond by pretending not to know that it is being surveilled. It may be in its best interests to feign ignorance. Finally, it may not know that it is being observed at all. The point is that whoever looks has more power than the one looked at. The point is also that the one who gazes seeks both control and knowledge. To control the object observed by looking at it and thereby scrutinising it is to gain knowledge about and, thereby, power over the one observed.

John Orr makes the point that the power of the gaze has properties in common with the power of surveillance.[28] The camera, as a technological instrument, has grown up as part of the culture of surveillance. What is more, camera technology, including that used in war technology, has turned the weapon into a gaze. For example, tanks use the periscopic anamorphic lens to gain 180-degree vision – it can see the enemy ahead, and from left to right.[29] Further still, the gaze has also been turned into a weapon as with infra-red telescopic lenses which allow the gazer to pick out his target in the dark and shoot to kill (as at the beginning of *Nikita*). Remember also the 'smart' video bombs used in the Gulf War that sent back images of successful target raids. The camera, then, is a technological device with death in its sights. And this camera technology is the one that also operates as the cinematic apparatus. The anamorphic lens brought cinema-scope on to the film screens. The camera operates as a supreme surveiller, bringing to the screen narratives of other people's lives that we can watch unseen. We gaze upon the screen and derive pleasure. The gaze is still a weapon. As with the camera as instrument of surveillance and war technology, it functions still as an agent of voyeurism and fetishism, only this time, more explicitly, pleasure in viewing is involved.

It would be useful to contextualise briefly how the system of the gaze and pleasure in viewing functions in mainstream narrative cinema, particularly in relation to these concepts of voyeurism

28 Orr (1993) 59.
29 *Ibid.*, 77.

and fetishism. Laura Mulvey in her powerful essay on visual pleasure makes the point that, in relation to film, there are basically three points of the gaze.[30] The three looks are that of the camera, the look within the film, and the spectator's. In mainstream cinema all three looks are traditionally perceived as male. The filmmaker/cameraman behind the camera's eye is traditionally male. The gaze within the film is agenced by the male protagonist who looks at the female. The female is positioned to be looked at and this in turn constructs the spectator psychically as male looking at the female, thereby deriving pleasure from looking and rendering the female fetish. This is the primary effect of the construction of the gaze in mainstream cinema. Since Mulvey's seminal essay of the mid-1970s, the debates around the gender of the gaze, particularly that of the spectator, have developed. How, after all, could a female spectator derive pleasure from such a positioning 'as male' unless she adopted either a masochistic positioning (identifying with the female passive/fetishised role) or that of a transvestite (identifying with the male active hero). Both women and men spectators derive pleasure in viewing so it is not possible ultimately to position the spectator so rigidly in relation to sexual identity. What is possible is to postulate the bisexuality of the spectator's positioning where the spectator fluctuates between passive and active modes. This will become a useful key when discussing the pleasure derived from Besson's films, particularly by female spectators, where women characters are placed voyeuristically, and where male violence abounds – more on this later.

As a primary effect, as the discussion above makes clear, the camera in mainstream cinema operates as an apparatus of fetishisation and voyeurism. The camera is, as we have said, most traditionally an extension of the male eye/'I'. This effect, therefore, is far from innocent and needs explaining. In psychoanalytic terms, fetishisation and voyeurism refer to the scopic strategies adopted by the male to counter his fear of sexual difference (between himself and the female, sexual other) and the fear of castration which he feels as a result of that difference (the

30 Laura Mulvey (1989) *Visual and Other Pleasures*, London, Macmillan, 14–16.

woman 'lacks' a penis, the male 'assumes' she has been castrated).
Thus, adopting the strategy of voyeurism, he fixes the woman with
his gaze, investigates her body and therefore her sexuality with his
gaze. She is the object of his investigation and in that way he safely
contains her. As the object of his look and surveillance, meaning
is ascribed to her by him – he contains her difference. Fetishism,
on the other hand, is the strategy adopted to disavow difference.
The male seeks to find the 'hidden' phallus in the woman. This
fetishisation takes place by a fragmentation of the body and an
over-investment in the part of the body (or a piece of clothing) that
has been fragmented off: breasts, legs, shoes, slinky dresses, gloves,
etc. Ultimately, the purpose of this over-investment is to make
those parts figure as the missing phallus, through perceiving
them as perfection in and of themselves. The female form is
contained this time by a denial of difference.

As Orr says, the power of the gaze is 'largely negative and
reactive, a source of malaise'[31] – primarily it expresses a personali-
sation of the 'politics of paranoia'.[32] Much of the *film noir* and
thriller genres are sites of display of this politics of paranoia. But
they are representative of a politics of paranoia around male
sexuality – a sense of malaise with the self in relation to the female
who threatens, it would appear, to usurp the male power position.
The first major manifestation of this politics of paranoia, as
expressed in film genre, came primarily from Hollywood in the
form of the *film noir*, and coincided with World War Two and its
immediate aftermath of the cold war period. This was a time when
men returning from war found their traditional roles as bread-
winners and workers usurped by the female who had 'taken their
place' at the work front. These *films noirs* and thrillers are still very
much in vogue today and are particularly popular in France – so
we must presume that the politics of paranoia have not
disappeared. In Besson's film *Nikita*, for example, Nikita is under
constant surveillance. Even if the camera is not present it is
implicitly so. We do not know that Nikita is not always 'seen'. The
camera gaze need not just be visual it can be sonic too. So in her

31 Orr (1993) 81.
32 *Ibid.*, 80.

private life with Marco the camera may not be there (but who is to know?). It is highly probable, however, that if a camera is not present a listening device will be.

The voyeuristic and fetishistic practices to which Nikita is subjected, the excess of looking, do bespeak a malaise that is to do with the politics of paranoia. But it is also one which is closely aligned to the cult of technology. This cult takes numerous forms in Besson's films, all of which are aspects of fetishism. Let me briefly explain this idea before developing a second, related point around this cult of technology. Orr makes the point that in this age of information (rapid information thanks to technology) 'the cult of information worships to excess its own sophisticated technologies'.[33] The cult of information is more than just the system of rapid communication, it is also that of camera surveillance and the weaponry of surveillance. It is also about hierarchies of power: those who may look and know as opposed to those who may not. The gaze is about control, control of knowledge and a will to power. Thus, those empowered to look will punish the disempowered who seek to look. Consider for a moment what happens to computer hackers. They get sent to jail (or alternatively the bank they were trying to hack into employs them to defend their technological system). Technology means policing in the final analysis. The technological systems themselves need protection. Having projected our efficiency, or desire for efficiency, on to the technological object, we are then obliged to protect the object of our own imaginings. Thus, the cult of technology manifests itself through excess.

Technology is present to excess in Besson's films to the point of fetish value, in particular in *Nikita* and *Léon* – although *Le Grand Bleu* is festooned with technomobilia (diving equipment, underwater cameras, etc.). If Nikita is an extension of 'male' technology (watched and watching), then Léon is its embodiment – he literally dresses to kill at the end of the film. His body is adorned with the latest in the art of gun technology. At first he is display, he then becomes an embodied grenade; technology as fetish, body as altar. In terms of camera technology and its

33 *Ibid.*, 59.

sophisticated power to probe, to acquire knowledge/information – again this is a trope of Besson's work. Who is watching in *Le Dernier Combat*? There is no obvious intra-diegetic eye, so where is the eye that watches? In *Subway*, we are constantly made aware of the degree of surveillance – the screens in the métro police station are only the beginning. There is a powerful relay of looks between police and the underworld citizens and the particular objects of their pursuit. The observed observe in the full knowledge that they are observed. However, when they forget the fact of surveillance then they are lost. The roller-skater gets nabbed by the police inspector; Fred gets shot (perhaps fatally). Precisely the same things occur in *Nikita*. On her last mission to the Eastern European embassy, Nikita (cross-dressed as male) forgets that she is being observed. Her momentary amnesia costs her her 'life' (she has to remove herself). Mathilda, in *Léon*, forgets the basic panopticon principle of contemporary (policed/technological/ information) society that everyone watches everyone when she enters the DEA building – surely *the* site of surveillance – and is caught 'unawares' (blind to the fact that she is being seen) in the male lavatory!

This brings us to a second aspect of this cult of technology – that of technology and regression. Baudrillard's text on *The System of Objects* investigates our relationship with technology, suggesting that these objects, which are a projection of our imaginings, far from being measures of human progression are markers (although we repress this 'truth') of our own regressiveness.[34] He makes it clear that whilst we do not necessarily acknowledge this contradiction, nonetheless, this contradiction surfaces albeit in a different formulation. He explains this concealment and contradiction in the following way: 'Technological society thrives upon a tenacious myth, the myth of uninterrupted technical progress accompanied by a continuing moral "backwardness" of man relative thereto.'[35] Pursuing this point, he goes on to say: 'moral stagnation transfigures technical progress and turns it into the only certain value, and hence the ultimate authority of our society;

34 Baudrillard (1996).
35 *Ibid.*, 123.

by the same token, the system of production is absolved of all responsibility'.[36] Let me explain by way of an example. Why when a satellite launch fails and the whole piece of technology blows up on the observing screen does a disembodied voice calmly state 'we have a problem' and not declare that as a result of human error some phenomenal amount of dollars has just gone up in smoke? One plain answer is that by deresponsibilising the technology (the projection of our imaginings) we deresponsibilise ourselves. We hold on to a false consciousness of technological progress to disguise our own lack of moral progress and then when the technological object breaks down we can feel doubly absolved of the need to make progress – if technology cannot do it, then no more can we. We need and want technology to fail; because if it really does progress then so too must the system of human relations. Human relations in the sense of power relations would have to cease – and ideology has no interest in the consensual collusion between dominated and dominator changing since that is the social alchemy that keeps everything and everyone in their 'rightful' place.[37] Thus, as Baudrillard says, 'the present production system while working for real technological progress, at the same time opposes it'.[38]

Technology and technology's dysfunctionality are therefore necessary socio-psychologically. But they are also necessary socio-economically. Just as power relations recycle themselves as always the same (dominator/dominated) so too technology recycles itself. Why, for example, was the concept of built-in obsolescence created around car technology? Clearly so that after so many miles (or kilometres) the owner of a car would either have to replace the parts or replace the car. If technology is a system of progress, surely a car should not start to encounter breakdowns in its parts as rapidly as it does? After all, cars built before this concept still have fluid working parts (even though they are now obsolescent as fast vehicles of transport). It is equally evident, then, that the

36 Ibid.

37 See Pierre Bourdieu's thoughts on the social construction of power relations in Bourdieu (1984) 318ff.

38 Baudrillard (1996) 124.

circulation of objects – including the fetishisation of objects (the BMW over the Mercedes) which is part of our desire to consume – also plays a key role in keeping us in our 'rightful' place. Some of us can afford to replace the old with the new version of the same (a new car). Others will replace broken parts with new or reconditioned parts depending on what they can afford.

When Baudrillard suggests that 'the ambition of objects [is] to act as replacements for human relationships' and that objects and technics can be perceived 'as substitute answers to human conflicts',[39] he is in essence talking about the principle of displacement and containment – in other words, we transfer on to technology our desires and our fears. In his discussion of automation and robots he makes this point abundantly clear. On our fascination with and desire to perfect automation, he makes the point that 'the degree to which a machine approaches perfection is everywhere presented as proportional to its degree of automatism'.[40] But, in this process of automating, we sacrifice a great deal of potential functionality. Automation represents a closing off on both the technical and the human level. Automation-as-perfection closes off the possibility for technical advances and closes out human beings in that it reduces them to the status of mere spectator. We watch our automated objects function in our place. This closing out of course deresponsibilises us, but at the same time we believe in the value of automation for 'the uses of automation mean a wondrous absence of activity, and the enjoyment of this process is comparable to that derived, on another plane, from seeing without being seen'.[41] We watch the fruits of our imaginings and because 'the automated object "works by itself", its resemblance to the autonomous human being is unmistakable, and the fascination thus created carries the day. We are in the presence of a new anthropomorphism.'[42] We watch it doing what we would do – the technical object is the projection of our efficiency, it is 'as our own image'.[43]

39 *Ibid.*, 125.
40 *Ibid.*, 110.
41 *Ibid.*, 111.
42 *Ibid.*
43 *Ibid.*

The heightened form of this anthropomorphisation is, of course, the robot – first imagined in sci-fi literature and now in 'existence'. In its ability to fulfil many tasks, the robot attests to 'man's phallic reign over the world'.[44] At the same time it is 'visibly an object, hence a *slave*'.[45] And as such the robot is dominated by man, and more significantly rendered asexual. The robot 'attests to a phallus that is enslaved'.[46] However, there is a paradox here. For, in that the robot is made in man's (*sic*) own image it is, ultimately, a projection of his subjectivity, that is, his sexuality. A robot is everything except sex, but, since it is a projection and containment of man's own subjectivity, it is an enslaved sexuality. Baudrillard argues that in this way a threatening part of man's self has been 'exorcised and turned into a sort of all-powerful slave'[47] – in other words, the creation of the robot is a way of man projecting his fear of the self. It becomes a means whereby man can displace his own fear of his sexuality (his sex-ness) and contain it (as a-sexual) – safe, neutralised and domesticated and outside of his self.

But what happens when the nightmare 'comes true' and the robot revolts (as all slaves in man's mythic world of terror must do)? We recall HAL in Stanley Kubrick's *2001 A Space Odyssey*. This robotic computer revolts against the cold rationality of the astronaut and attempts to take over the space mission. Not only does he fail, it is the way in which he fails that matters. He is smashed to pieces in a pyrotechnic finale by his 'creator'. Man's relation to the robot is a fraught one. Although the robot is a slave, implicit in that concept is the notion that 'he' may revolt, that everything which 'he' embodies (subjugated sexuality) will break out and turn against man. This is a frequent trope of science fiction, as we know. Man's solution is to seek the fragmentation or death of the robot, and in sci-fi films this is particularly spectacularised and relished (the spectator enjoys seeing the robot either go off the rails or being 'beaten to death'). This destruction

44 *Ibid.*, 121.
45 *Ibid.*, 120.
46 *Ibid.*, 121.
47 *Ibid.*

is not just a moral closure, a denunciation of the evil powers of technology. Nor is it just about man's abuse of his scientific powers. It also represents the 'symbolic spectacle of (man's) atomization of his own sexuality – which he himself destroys, having pressed it into the service of his own image'.[48] And Baudrillard concludes: '[i]f we carry the Freudian view to its logical conclusion, we cannot but wonder whether this is not man's way of using technology in its most demented incarnation to celebrate the future occurrence of his own death, his way of renouncing his sexuality in order to be quit of all anxiety'.[49] The use and 'abuse' of technology here is then twofold. First, it is a regressive move to control the libido and put an end to sexuality (a form of death of course), and in its destruction it represents a move to spectacularise death – make it visible – so as to control it. A *mise-en-scène* of our death instinct in other words.

Viewed in this light, technology becomes our imaginary death: it is a projection of the temptation man feels to regress towards 'death as an escape from sexual anxiety'.[50] Because objects and technics are victims of in-built obsolescence, technology manifests itself as serial death: we daily watch our death, but we do not experience it. Because of the object's ability to fail we are ultimately spared that regressive move towards death. When an object fails, in much the same way as we discussed with the robot, it is as if it has revolted (refused to work). At first we are angered by its failure ('my car just died'), but then we accept the 'inevitable' and read this failure 'as evidence of a fragility that distinctly appeals to us'.[51] What would our reaction be, Baudrillard asks, if an object were infallible – it would, he argues, be a renewed source of anxiety. The infallibility of the object pointing to our very real obsolescence (death). Thanks to the death of the object our own sexuality can resurface, however briefly, and life goes on.

To rephrase Baudrillard, the cult of technology then points to the dysfunctionality of our present social structures which are

48 *Ibid.*, 122.
49 *Ibid.*
50 *Ibid.*, 132.
51 *Ibid.*, 131.

based in the capitalist order of production and the capitalist imperative to consume (serially and seriously). The cult represents a projection outward of a social malaise that conceals the very real conflicts inherent in individual and social relations.[52] And this brings us back to considerations of Besson's work. Whilst he uses technology in excess, his films reveal a profound ambivalence towards the power of this technology – including of course the camera, the technology of surveillance *par excellence*. Two of his characters at least, Nikita and Léon, are visual embodiments of the fetishistic value of this cult of technology. They are both programmed to kill, commanded to by the voice of technology in the case of Nikita, paid to in the case of Léon. They are both human automatons, highly efficient – robots of the highest quality (degree 'n') endowed with the best technology of death that man can supply. The State sits back and watches Nikita at work – the automatised State-killer at work – fascinated by her skillfulness. It sees without being seen. Léon is the only witness (apart from us and the camera of course) to his own exterminating skills. But his precision is never in doubt, any more than his exemplary efficiency and clean ways (not a wasted shot). Both characters 'revolt' and die for it. Nikita, who was supposed to disappear in a pyrotechnic display 'à la Rambo' in an earlier version of the script, still disappears and the circumstances in which she makes her chosen exit are violent enough even if it is Victor the robotic cleaner who gets destroyed – shot to pieces in the shoot-out. Her revolt is a form of death (gone forever). Léon (embodied by Jean Reno who played Victor, so robots can re-emerge, be recycled) is an asexual, domesticated automaton (witness his patterned behaviour with his plant), who obeys on command (shoots to order). That is until Mathilda enters his world and becomes the life-force that triggers his revolt. He becomes a smart, intellectualised robot, he learns to read and write. As we have seen, if you give a robot a brain you are well on the route to revolt (remember HAL). A feeling, thinking robot cannot survive, for the very reasons invoked above: it is too close to the real to be tolerated, and so must die. Preferably in spectacular fashion.

52 *Ibid.*, 132.

Besson's films as the *mise-en-scène* of this cult of technology and commodified capitalism

Technology and the body: death violence and display

Besson's representation, in his films, of consumer commodities as signs of death (for example, the graveyard of cars and floating washing machines in an abandoned car factory in *Le Dernier Combat*) and his fascination with flotsam and the recycling of objects can be read as metaphors for the fact that we live in the era of post-industrial decay. If this is the case, then Besson's films are clear suggestions that any attempt to use objects and technics as substitute answers to human conflicts is a futile exercise in displacement and containment, even though it is one which we practise. Indeed, Besson's films can be read as exposures of this practice through their investigations of the interface between technology and the body and the environments (cities, underground, underwater). His films are a *mise-en-scène* of the way in which violent interactions are played out between the three, as well as violence within the body as a site/sight of technology. Display, voyeurism, performativity, transgression and violence are key ways of discussing these issues.

Display and excess are fundamental aspects of Besson's characters' performance. Is Léon's violence an escape from his dysfunctionality – as represented through the five degrees of his infantilisation – or is it a symptom and display of that dysfunctionality? Is it both? He is already doubly displaced as an Italian living in the USA and a giant in the dwarfed (by name) 'Little Italy' area of New York City. He is held in scope, vertically pressed down upon by the lines of the frame and the lines of the cityscape. The five-time infantilised Léon collides with the automatised contract killer producing a safe, because asexual, man-child. Contained as such, he stands as a feminised phallus who has to strap the guns on to his body, like a prosthesis. His body is ornamented by the phallus, is not the phallic itself. His violence is fetishistic, even acrobatic, display of the phallic object – that which replaces male sexuality, places it outside the body. This is why Mathilda disturbs, because in her various declarations of love she is asking him, however inappropriate on her part it might seem, to reclaim the phallus. As a feminised phallus, Léon is the manifest inverse of what the male protagonist of a gangster film should signify – or what mainstream cinema portrays him as signifying. Léon enters the zone *of* and masquerades *as* the fetishised female of *film noir*. Or put another, baudrillardian way, he becomes what man both admires and fears most. He becomes the robot that fascinates through its efficiency but which threatens as the reflection of man's phallic mastery over the world. Léon masquerades through technological adornment as the automated robot we gaze upon. He becomes his own embodied projection, an auto-constructed robot which is nothing short of a self-fulfilling death-wish (man destroys the robotised self/other) since we recall that, unable to tolerate the threat of the robot, man will annihilate it. Viewed in this logic, Léon has to auto-destruct.[53] Léon's body becomes, then, the site of that tension between sexuality, identity and the fear of death which he resolves in a cataclysmic way: the body as self-projected technological object blows up.

In *Le Dernier Combat*, the first representation of the body is that of the female as an inflatable doll which an adult male, the lead protagonist, is 'screwing'. A good metaphor for the interfacing between object/technics and the human body if ever there was one! This display of male sexuality in a vacuum is rapidly followed by the protagonist's attempt to escape the violent attack of other males as he takes off in a single propelled plane he has built himself. The plane is recycled from waste. The protagonist's clothing is recycled from waste. He takes off only to crash in the desert – the wasteland *par excellence* (at least in western mythology). He has managed to move from one derelict city to another, there is no distinction. The one could as easily be the other. When he steps outside, it rains fish – tons of dead fish – a consumer product that will last only until it too rots and decays. Waste in excess. Waste, decay, dereliction. That is his environment. The message seems clear. To invest technics and objects with the power of signifying as answers to human conflicts means surely that such a process

53 There are other readings to this death by self-explosion and I will address them in the next chapter.

must eventually backfire and turn around on itself and return the destructive image to man of his refusal to evolve. And return it as decay, dereliction and waste. The anthropomorphised objects hit back and refuse to act as replacements for human relationships. Thus, violence – the pathology of the repressed – breaks out. The doctor is stoned to death, the marauder is eventually killed by the lead protagonist, as are other males who are in his way. This trajectory of his is not for some high-minded principle, but to gain supremacy over another male (indeed series of males) so that he can take the woman. In other words, this *flâneur* of dereliction has been forced to resume the basic human instinct: sex. But this is hardly a great *mise-en-scène* of hope. Given the derelict environment which he inhabits, even if he is successful in reproducing, there is little evidence to suppose that there exists a social order of things into which he could reproduce. The city is laid waste. So is man's future.

What is also interesting in this film is the complete sense of deresponsibilisation that is manifest at all levels of human comportment. The narrative context is science fiction: the space we project our 'worst' fantasies into – or our most advanced imaginings. Science fiction is the ultimate expression in imaginary projection, says Baudrillard.[54] It is the generic form of deregulated deresponsibilisation: automation/technology, in or out of control, is neither man's nor the object's responsibility. Whether the object functions or fails, it conveniently stands in for our repressed fears. The city also figures importantly in the sci-fi genre and reflects through its representation another panoply of man's repressed fears. The city is after all the ultimate expression of society's political embodiment. It is the site of power (political, economic, religious, etc.); it is also the site of repression (policing, surveillance, etc.) and subversion (revolt, strikes, sedition, intellectual dissent, terrorism, etc.). Finally, it is the site in which much of human pathology finds an outlet (crime, prostitution, murder). The city, over this last century, has also been the primary stake in war – whether it has been merely 'taken', or bombed to the point of total dereliction. When taken, as with Paris in World

54 Baudrillard (1996) 119.

War Two, the city is occupied by a foreign body – an image of rape or looting by the alien-other comes to mind. When bombed, the city is laid to waste: not just buildings but also human bodies (Hiroshima, Nagasaki, London, Dresden, the major cities of ex-Yugoslavia are just a few examples). The imagined city in science fiction is often monstrous, technology having created buildings of 'appalling' power (as in Lang's *Metropolis* or Scott's *Blade Runner*). Alternatively, as with *Le Dernier Combat*, it has been reduced to the degree zero. In both instances the city environments are represented as extremes and we witness behaviour from the inhabitants that reflects those extremes. The environment now becomes the site of display, the outlet for the worst of human pathology, precisely because the city as body politic has either disappeared (as in Besson's film) or has been reinscribed into a new order that fetishises technology, a new order that is a megalopolis and believes only in reproduction (as in *Blade Runner*). These two extremes, dereliction and fetishism, are projections of our worst fears: the death of society, that is, our own death as a result of technological excess and absolute capitalism. They are fears displaced outside the self. As we explained with the robot, science fiction is the *mise-en-scène* of our most irrational fears but it is also a form of absolving ourselves from any responsibility for progress within the social order of things. The subtextual reading of science fiction becomes then the following. Not to participate in the evolution of the social order is to suscribe to the ultimate destruction of the social body and the body politic. Man causes his own alienation and dereliction. However, he seems incapable of taking this idea on board. So he looks outside, fascinated by the technology he has made but which he disavows (by refusing any responsibility for its excess). Man looks outside, perceives himself as victim of the saturation effect of the very objects he has designed, victim to his own fetish. He is assailed by the aesthetics of advertising which cajole him to both reproduce objects and consume more. The sci-fi environment then is the pathological universe of our future. Consume and die.

There are a number of ironic presences in *Le Dernier Combat* pointing to our practice of reproduction and consumption of technological goods. First, the advertising boards for the electrical goods company Darty, which sells on the advertising slogan that its prices cannot be beaten, points to what can no longer be consumed. In this wasteland all meccas of consumerism have been destroyed (this one is literally underwater). The actual environments Besson chooses as his sets are further ironic presences. The disused Citroën factory at Balard points to the end of the motor industry, the derelict EDF factory to the end of light and power. Nothing works, nothing can be made: the system of objects and our pathological dependence on them has broken down. So what happens to our repressed fears which had this former pathological outlet? In Besson's film, we are beyond the fallibility of the object. The object simply is no more. And yet the refusal to take responsibility is there as strong as ever before. The doctor, who is arguably the most 'humanitarian' of all the survivors of the holocaust and who draws on walls like a cave-man (reproducing the myth of Adam and Eve) and who almost speaks, is the one who comes closest to an embodiment of the earlier social order of things. He believes in life, in procreation, otherwise why would he protect the woman from one type of marauding male and endeavour to find her the ideal partner in the form of the wounded protagonist? But he believes in life on his terms. He chooses who will procreate. So he reproduces hierarchies of power, albeit in a vacuum. He also suggests the idea of genetic selection – he will present the female only with a suitable male. The derelict city is a threatening space, where predators scavenge and kill for an existence and privatise space or the rare commodities that still exist (water). The doctor has the 'hospital', the gang leader the sewage pipes. Again hierarchies of power are reproduced, suggesting that human beings have no other knowledge. Ideology is recycling itself to death. The city is beyond dystopia. It is beyond belief – no hope for utopia here. It too is the sphere of death.

Le Dernier Combat is a metaphor for the death of ideology. It is also a metaphor for our living death. The film shows us what we already know but refuse to acknowledge, preferring instead to transmogrify death by projecting it on to technology and subsequently willing its death. And the film shows us how we deny that knowledge through social, cultural and sexual regression – which leads, ultimately, to the death of the sexual, social and political body. This first film of Besson's is arguably his most politicised one. I would argue, however, that his subsequent films take up the same issues but develop them less phatically and within a broader framework of human comportment. For example, transgressiveness is far more marked in subsequent characterisations in Besson's films even though, at the same time, these openly transgressive types paradoxically remain for the most part sexually regressive. I've spoken about the complex play with violence and identity in Léon's characterisation, but what about Fred, Nikita, Jacques? All dysfunctional, transgressive-regressive types who disappear.

Transgressiveness is a 'punishable' offence. The trope of *film noir* is that the transgressive female is the one who is identified as sexually active. She is the one who will be probed and investigated. In mainstream cinema, active female sexuality is, then, perceived as a moral transgression. What of the male? Where does his trans-gressiveness lie? Often in the opposite direction: inactive male sexuality. The male, in his refusal to fulfil the Oedipal trajectory, is perceived as morally transgressive. In other words, sexual regress-iveness in the male is transgressive. Neither Jacques (in *Le Grand Bleu*) nor Fred (in *Subway*) are seeking to fulfil their assigned trajectory with any urgency. Fred dies as much as a result of his fascination for music as for Héléna. Instead of running from his pursuers, he deliberately focuses on his main ambition to get a rock group started. And it is because he wishes to gaze upon that triumph that he gets shot, not because he gazes upon Héléna. One could argue that he puts music before her and that indeed having once seduced Héléna into the underworld it is now she who actively seeks him out. Fascinated by his own creation (the band) he neglects to think that he too may be being watched. This fascination with the object of his creation makes him blind to the danger that surrounds him, a blindness for which he will be 'punished'. His transgressive behaviour (his voyeuristically watch-ing the band, his own fetish, and not the woman, the traditional object of the gaze) puts him on display to the predatory, surveilling and phallic eye. He is unintentionally, unwittingly hiding in the light. Thus, in terms of the sexually active and inactive, Fred dies as much from Héléna's decision not to reject him (female active sexuality) as from his own decision to fulfil his dream (male inactive sexuality). His love of music puts him in the light and he gets killed; but at the same time her love of him puts him in the light and makes him the target that must be killed. The stolen documents are history really, it is more the avenging and jealous husband who issues Fred's death warrant to his hit-men than the man who has had his secret and possibly damaging documents purloined. It is as if the display of transgressiveness is double: Fred's and Héléna's. She who 'wants' too much, he who wants too little.

In *Le Grand Bleu*, Jacques' major transgression is to desire the siren of the sea, the dolphin, more than the siren of the land, Johana. When he has an orgasm making love with the earth-woman Johana he thinks of the sea and the dolphin, not the woman who is desperately trying to unite with him and tie him down to fulfilling his oedipal trajectory. He refuses to be landed, choosing to rejoin his sea-mother-lover and find death in a transcendent way rather than stay within a social order of things that fixes him to an earth-mother and keeps him on dry land where he is so clearly lost. Even Johana's announcement that he has successfully impregnated her is not enough to hold him back. His transgressive display is threefold. He is the dolphin, the man-dolphin. He loves the dolphin, the female dolphin he had earlier helped to set free, and loves her more than the earth-woman. Finally, he chooses death over life – the very thought man cannot abide. His behaviour, then, is completely counter-oedipal – and one might say about time too (at least in terms of film theory), for it is not necessarily a negative choice. Jacques is offering a counter-message. Contrary to the example given by Enzo who dies for it, there is an alternative to the competitive race of life. One can choose death, as Jacques does, as an act that makes sense. There is an alternative to the social order of things. Contrary to Johana's initial desire to keep Jacques in the social sphere, it could be argued that Jacques, by impregnating Johana (as she had so fervently wished) and leaving her to reproduce, refuses to buy into the whole myth of 'marriage', stability and family life. And even if this message is misogynistic in its resonances, we have to remember that Johana helps to let Jacques go – she literally releases him into the sea. So she colludes in his escape from the oedipal trajectory, having at first tried to entrap him within it. Jacques leaves a life (his unborn child) and he takes a life (his own). An equitable exchange. No excess, no waste.

In *Le Grand Bleu*, the safe environment is the sea. The land is the space of predatory men and women. Predatory men of capitalist enterprise and scientific endeavour, these are the landmen who are in pursuit of the dream of excellence and capitalism – absolute capitalism. Dive deeper, they exclaim enticingly, act as display-bodies (as opposed to display-cabinets) for our capitalist enterprising endeavours and we will double your prize money. A man's body can be bought for a price/prize. Win, but promote our product: capitalism. Women are frivolous extras that sap man's strength, there is not one to be seen underwater at least not in earthly form. They want money or babies – two forms of reproduction, the one strictly capitalist, the other the embodiment of capitalist ideology: produce to consume.

Once we perceive the film in this light we can begin to understand its own inherent violence – and it becomes more than just the New Age movie for which it has been dismissed by some critics (even though this does not mean to say that it is a totally satisfactory film, as I argued in the previous chapter). If we can leave aside the misogyny as it is displayed around women (from Enzo's Italian mother to Johana) – at least for a moment (or the next chapter) – then we can see that there are issues around maleness and technology being played out in this film that need serious attention. Jacques puts his body at the service of science: he goes to Peru and there, at high altitude, he free-dives for scientists to measure effects on the body, most particularly the heart. Later on in the film, both Jacques and Enzo go to the North Sea to participate in further experiments on the effects of pressure on the brain – this time they are placed in a capsule (with a stereotypically humourless Belgian) – so the human effort is not theirs, which might explain why they deliberately sabotage the experiment by getting drunk on the job. In both instances, however, the body is made available to science and in exchange provides Jacques and then Enzo with the wherewithall to pursue their own dreams: free-diving, the one to feel free and to meet up with his dolphins (Jacques), the other to prove he is the best (Enzo). It is instructive that Jacques does not need technology to assist him, he merely meditates through his body and is then ready to dive. Enzo, on the other hand, is all blow and bluster before he goes down, and he pushes aside technology and scientific advice even though it could save his life. The men of science, who have paid these free-divers to assist them in pushing forward the boundaries of scientific knowledge, are powerless, however, to put a stop to what they have begun. Aided and abetted by the mediatic pressure and the capitalist pressure of the entrepreneurs, they allow the final and fatal free-diving com-petition to take place – it is too late when they announce that the human body literally cannot go below the very depth Enzo is willing his body to achieve. But Enzo dies as much a victim of his own ambition, his own dream to be the best, his own machismo, as he does an investigative probe of science (he probes the depths of tolerance). In this respect, he is both subject and object of his death. Meantime of course the camera technology voyeuristically gazes on. It too plumbs the depths, observing the body that is s/training for its moment of perfection. In the end, Enzo rejects what technology can offer (the medics at the last marker who advise him to resurface) and passes beyond it – the camera remains behind unable or unwilling to follow, electing to observe at a distance the floating, now dead object of its gaze. Jacques will follow, but there will be no technology there to help (the place is closed down), only the camera to watch as he disappears from view.

We have moved beyond the idea of gender transgressiveness as sexual transgression (active female/inactive male) to a notion of the transgressive male body pure and simple. If technology is our outer projection, the displacement and containment of our fear of death, then both Jacques and Enzo – but in particular Jacques –

are embodiments of a new line of transgression. Theirs is the trajectory towards death we constantly seek and yet constantly seek to avoid. The point is that whereas man seeks to regress towards death as a way of avoiding sexual anxiety, here both characters have gone beyond that regressive motivation. In other words, there is no fear of sex in their trajectory, but there is a challenge to technology and capitalism. Clearly, in both cases, their actions question the power of technology and the wisdom of scientists that says there are limits to human endeavour that only science and technology can assert and impose. Their actions also question the displacement on to technology of our death-wish and our attempts to use technology as a substitute answer for our inability to resolve human relations. Their act of rejecting technology is to embrace death (because fear of it is no longer projected out on to the technics) and forego human relationships.

The difference between the two characters' death is, of course, the motivation. Enzo knows he may die for his effort at record-breaking. But his boundary breaking behaviour is motivated by the desire not to lose, to be number one. The violence he does to himself, to his body, is motivated then by a principle that has guided western culture from the start: aggressive competition – a foundation stone of capitalism. So he is transgressive within the system, the social order of things. Jacques's transgression on the other hand is outside the system. It is one that cannot be recuperated and made sense of by the social order of things. He rejects the socialised adult and his belief in the effectiveness of technology as a substitute for human progress. His transgression makes the point, rather, that there is no progress to be had. Jacques' motivation is self-less, an effortless relinquishing of male subjectivity, a giving-up the self. As such his motivation is non-sexualised bliss, the bliss of being in another order of things which Besson describes as disappearing, a state of non-being (see Chapter Two). Jacques, in the final analysis, breaks the earth-bounding effect of limits (which say you must go no further and you must return to land) and returns the body to its place of origin. A kind of genesis in reverse. The body has reunited with the sea, 'la mer/mère'. The fantastic impossibility of reunification in the

Imaginary with the mother occurs at the precise moment of entry into bliss, 'jouissance', the Real Order that is beyond sex and close, very much so, to the unspeakable and unrepresentable moment of death. In this respect and in relation to the fetishising effect of the cult of technology, the message of this film is a utopian one: the rejection of technology and acclamation through the body of the 'death-bliss'.

Technology and the body: transgression, voyeurism and the postmodern subject as cyborg

To a degree, Jacques and Léon are fortunate in that they get to agence (be the subject of) their own effacement. Not so Nikita, hence the more deeply pessimistic resonances of that film. It must be said too that in relation to *Nikita* gender transgressiveness is back on the agenda, and it cannot be entirely pure happenstance that this is so and that the central protagonist is a woman. We also recall that Besson made it clear that in his own mind gender issues were at stake in this film – particularly the supposed inacceptability, socially, of women's expression of violence. To all intents and purposes then Besson's film is about the social containment of woman. My own feeling is that there are more deeply hidden agendas that are not entirely free of misogyny. And the following analysis of this film needs to be read in the light of this dual perspective.

Earlier in this chapter, I raised the issue of female spectator-ship in relation to pleasure in viewing. And this will be my starting point for this discussion of *Nikita*. Much of the female audience of *Nikita* perceive the central character positively and read her story as a trajectory towards freedom. However, if we unpack the representation of Nikita it becomes difficult to read her trajectory positively and I want to argue that there seems to be a gap between representation and perception. In other words, there is a gap between what appears to be represented and which gives visual pleasure (Nikita as transgressive and obtaining freedom) and what is actually represented. My contention is that the film – either intentionally or not, because Besson may well have meant to expose this process – through its apparent seamlessness allows visual pleasure to override the more deep-rooted meaning of this film which is containment, that is, using the female body as a displaced figure of masculinity.

This issue first exposes itself if we stop to consider how spectator-positioning functions in this film. The film is all about surveillance, about the camera apparatus as instrument of observation, permanent visibility and therefore repression. The film apparatus makes the audience the eye of the camera. And that eye is far from neutral, for it positions us as male and/or the State (because Nikita is continuously under State surveillance). So we are positioned as male, the State even, never as female. Where then does the female spectator find herself located in this pleasure in viewing?

As with female spectatorship and the tradition of *film noir*, *Nikita* provides a double-bind situation for female spectators – or, alternatively, we could argue that it exposes that double-bind. First, in identifying with Nikita as a positive image for women (as transgressive and obtaining freedom) we must accept all sorts of violations to our sense of identity. Nikita is annihilated and remade as Marie/Joséphine; she is subjected to the orders of the State; her freedom is to end up as absence. This 'acceptance' positions the female spectator masochistically. By identifying with and taking pleasure in viewing Nikita, we view 'our' own subjection and approve of it. Thus, a first order of violence enters into play: the female body as the object of violence in and of itself. Nikita confirms the erasure of her own identity by disappearing.

Second and conversely, in reading the representation of Nikita as a negative image of woman we again encounter a problem. That negative image is one that contains woman (a trope of *film noir* of course), one that makes the female body safe by fetishising it. Woman becomes phallic, undifferentiated from and therefore unthreatening to the male. Female sexuality is denied, through the very images that purport to represent her (Nikita dressed in fetishistic mode with the slinky black dress, stilleto heels, black gloves and the gun). This time the female spectator implicitly occupies a sadistic position. She adopts, however temporarily, the position of the male voyeur. Thus her own sexuality, at best, is held in suspension – at worst, denied. A second order of violence, therefore, enters into play – again located around the female body.

However, this is not the audience-position female spectators perceive themselves to be occupying when watching *Nikita*. This implies that the representation of Nikita's transgressiveness is sufficient to suggest that she never loses consciousness of her ability to revolt even if that revolt is always, in the final analysis, contained. It is then the spectacle of transgression that gives pleasure, not the containment of it afterwards. Let us now look at three instances of Nikita's transgressiveness and show how her embodiment of feminine disruption is an attraction, but also make the point that there are other factors at work here.

The first example of transgression concerns cross-dressing and gender unfixity. At two points in the film at least, Nikita crosses gender boundaries. In the opening sequence, she is part of a raid on a chemist's shop with several other drug addicts. In her dress-code and gestures she is unfixed as gender: she is woman-child/boy-man as she sits foetally toting a gun which she then uses to kill a cop. Towards the end of the film she 'returns' to her earlier transgressiveness when she purposely cross-dresses, dresses like a man, to accomplish her mission (an espionage raid on a foreign embassy). Although she acquires the documentation, her disguise fails – the surveillance cameras pick her up and the guards realise s/he is not the embassy diplomat. S/he is uncovered. She escapes and Victor gets wiped out in a flurry of gunfire. To all intents and purposes, this is the last we see of her – she says goodbye to Marco and after that she disappears, has to disappear as her only way out of the killing cycle. The price she has to pay to get out is absence. It is instructive that immediately after these two moments when she cross-dresses or is unfixed as gender she has to occupy a place of 'not-being'. The first time round (at the beginning of the film) Nikita gets 'killed off', the second time she disappears. In the first instance, she challenges the social order of things and their boundaries; in the second, she embodies the collapse of gender boundaries. In both cases she disrupts identity and order – and for that, it would appear, she gets consigned to absence.

The notion of transgression as excess and its subsequent repression seem to be at work here. We recall our earlier comments about this in relation to youth in crisis and its commodification as transgressive by the representatives of the social order of things. In fact, the whole film could be said to be a play between transgression and repression, with Nikita as the transgressive youth in crisis and Bob as the representative of the State and the repressive social order of things. And undoubtedly part of the appeal of this film is the rewriting of the David and Goliath myth in which, this time, violent youth (Nikita) is pitted against the socialised adult (Bob). Bob represents law and order – male, patriarchal order. He is the man of the State/Secret Police/patriarchy, and as such he represents the centre, the law of the father. In this respect, he embodies the centre, the social order of things that excludes the female Nikita as subject. That is, she is held or holds herself outside. His is a body that matters (has substance within the law), hers not – this is why in the end she can be remoulded/remodelled. Nikita, when we first meet her, represents or, rather, is represented as all that is the opposite of Bob. She is wild, disorderly, what is outside the law, what is not controllable. She is represented as breaking bounds, issuing challenges to the law. She starts off then as an embodiment of a complete negation of patriarchal law, of the ruling norms. Now, part of that patriarchal law is the definition of femininity's position of 'otherness'. To explain: as 'other' (sexually different), the woman defines the self, male subjectivity: the self, the subject of patriarchal law. That is, her sexual difference marks her as distinct from the male. The male looks at her and sees himself as whole (having the phallus), the female as lack; and is thus reassured of his sexual wholeness, unity. Within this law, male subjectivity depends on the 'otherness' of the female to affirm his unified subjectivity. When woman represents lack (as in good, pure and helpless) she does not threaten. When she represents excess (as in dangerous, chaotic and seductive) then she becomes what man fears most. As lack she is less than man, as excess she is more. As excess she no longer returns the image of the unified subjectivity of the male. She becomes a threat to his sex. As one might expect, it is this chaotic, seductive and dangerous woman who must disappear. Nikita (like so many *film noir* heroines before her) meets with the fate of the unruly, chaotic and seductive woman of excess. She disappears because her transgressiveness is one that crosses and dissolves gender boundaries – she threatens the very thing that secures masculinity (the binary gender division).

A second aspect of her transgressiveness concerns her 're-birth', her recycling by Bob into an instrument of the State. When she becomes the State-killer, undoubtedly we (as female specta-tors) experience some satisfaction, pleasure at her successful completion of her mission. When, however, she botches her last mission, I would argue that in this instance her performance causes us unpleasure – fear. It is noteworthy that her botching occurs at her moment of performativity as cross-dressed, so she undoes the double pleasure we could have experienced at her transgressiveness. Instead of being successful in her mission *and* cross-dressed, she fails. She fails, is made to fail because she has truly transgressed and broken the rules of the cultural construction of femininity. Let me explain. As State-killer she is reborn to embody the *femme fatale*. This she does successfully in her first mission with her fetishistic iconography. But remember she has been 'dressed up' as such under the ever-watchful eye of Bob who, with the assistance of Amande, has reconstructed her as feminine. She embodies the male construction of the *femme fatale* as deceptive masquerade: she looks like a woman but she is fetishised as phallic (the dress, shoes, gloves and gun over-invest parts of the body over the whole and contain her safely as phallic). In a sense, she is doubly fetish. First, through the convention of over-investment in parts of her body (a trope of *film noir*), and second because she 'truly' is a male-made female. Bob has reborn her. She is his imagining, his reproduction (of life). And this is the fetish whom the State/Bob obliges to kill on its behalf. An interesting displacement of masculinity that recalls the function of robots. And a point worth developing briefly because it ties in with this question of the double fetishisation of her body.

As a cross between Bob's fictional creation and recycled living woman, Nikita is more than a robot *per se*, she is a cyborg – a hybrid of machine (the weaponry of death) and organism (the female body), a creature of fiction and social reality. We are not far from science fiction here and *Nikita* is in some respects a cyborg-cop movie. Nikita is a cyborg, a creation of Bob's fantasy. She is reborn of Bob-the-father which means removing the mother. We recall that at the beginning of the film Nikita 'dies', calling out for her lost mother. 'Maman' she calls out as she is given an injection she assumes is lethal. As an all-male creation she is reborn into an all-male environment of technology, electronic mass-media and surveillance. She is constantly under the eye of the State and lives, therefore, in an environment of total surveillance, suppression and repression. When she becomes a killer agent for the State, she is given a new name, Marie, and the code name Joséphine (for her murderous missions). She can have any name. It can be just as arbitrarily chosen as her first name, Nikita, which she chose from a song. Of course, none of these names are innocent: Nikita is a Russian name for a boy, Marie is the Virgin Mary and Joséphine is Napoléon's wife – as we all know.[55] But in the film they refer to nothing and the point is rather that these names are arbitrarily recycled just as Nikita is recycled from the waste that she was as a junkie. She is reproduced by the State and has a couple of name-tags slapped on to her. She has been recycled into an efficient State-assassin. Recycled to do male work, to handle male technology (as killer agent), the very technology that handles her (surveilles her). Recycled, efficient cyborg she may well be; but as we have seen in the case of other technic imaginings of man, she must also have built-in obsolescence. Whether she revolts or wears out, her time will be up either way.

In the meantime, the only way she can stay alive is by dealing out death on the orders from the State/Bob-the-father. She is no longer the agent of violence she was in the opening sequence. She has become the vehicle for and embodiment of State violence, a

55 The constant interruptions Nikita receives when being in bed or about to make love with Marco become quite amusing in the light of her code name Joséphine.

sadistic outcome of containment of woman as violent. The question now becomes, what is going on? Why is Nikita being projected as cyborg and fetish? And it is here that we can perceive the misogyny of the film seeping through the gaps. This is what I read as happening. As the site of State violence, Nikita masquerades as feminine; masquerades because she is already a male construct, a fetish – she is fetishistically contained as safe, the guns 'adorning' her body (some of which are bigger than her!) make sure there is no mistaking that her own sexuality is disavowed (the strategy of fetishism). But she masquerades as feminine also because she is the State/Bob's re-creation of the 'other'-as-same. That is, the female-other has been re-created as same, as phallic. She is man-made, the cyborg imagining, the projection of man's imaginings that does man's work, displays his skills in weaponry, does death in his sight and site (in his place). She is the performing phallus, but she is not the 'real' thing.[56] So she is doubly masquerading, doubly 'other'-as-same since she is both fetishised-as-phallic *and* made-as-phallic. And in terms of performativity she is then obliged to act phallically: the fetished-phallic acting as the phallus (acting as State-killer). She does man's violence for him – she thus deresponsibilises him of all actions that she perpetrates in his place.

Why is this so? To rephrase Laura Mulvey and her discussion of condensation and replacement (a mechanism whereby the unconscious disguises its thought), Nikita is the one repressed idea disguised as another.[57] And that repressed idea is the former Nikita, the one at the beginning of the film, the one that collapses gender boundaries, who is disguised as fetishised cyborg which then becomes Bob/the male's displaced 'phallus' at work. In containing her this way, Bob/the male can both disavow and represent the source of his anxiety: female difference and the fear of castration. By repressing Nikita and remaking her 'in his

56 We recall that in our discussion of *Léon* the main protagonist was feminised in relation to the phallic.
57 See Laura Mulvey's (1995) essay 'The Myth of Pandora: A Psychoanalytical Approach', in Laura Pietrapaolo and Ada Testaferri (eds) *Feminisms in the Cinema*, Bloomington and Indiana, Indiana University Press.

image' he disavows and contains her difference and disguises it as a projection of masculinity (the phallus made safe as fetish and cyborg) which he can then control. So, to return to Nikita's last effort at cross-dressing, we can see again why s/he must fail: by dressing as the male and passing for male (which s/he does to start with since she gains access to the embassy), s/he becomes the very *thing* Bob/the male is trying to disguise her as. She agences becoming what he has imagined her as: the fetishised phallus. In other words, she comes dangerously close to blowing his strategy apart.

But the game is more complex still than that because the masculine is using the feminine body as voyeur and killer. Nikita the State-killer only looks to shoot, and she does it under State/male orders – as one remarkable series of shots in this film makes clear when she is sent to Venice to kill a target. In this series of shots, Nikita is looking down a telescopic lens ready to fire on her target once she is told who it is (she is kept in ignorance at all times). The voice of the State (male) tells her to shoot the target, a woman. Just before she shoots, the camera (traditionally a male eye) looks down the telescopic lens into Nikita's eye, then out through the lens to the target whom Nikita 'removes'. The probe used by Nikita (the telescopic lens on the rifle with its camera-eye properties) is the displaced male probe. The masculine eye/I uses the female body as an instrument of voyeurism and death. This scene is a metaphor for the whole process of condensation and displacement being played out with Nikita's body. Here the masculine conceals, disguises his own investment in voyeurism by using the female body. Further still, what is also occurring is a displacement, on to the female object, of the male desire to remove the castrating female-'other'. The disguise is a clever one. By making the female the one doing the removing (the woman removes the woman), the feminine is represented as the one agencing death. However, in truth, the construction of the feminine functions here to disguise the anxiety caused by sexual difference and simultaneously disguises the process of displacement. The real point of the disguised meaning is the male desire for woman (here Nikita) to remove herself – which she does in the end.

However, there is another, related reason why she must disappear and this brings me to the third and last point on Nikita's transgressiveness as an attraction and its subsequent disavowal and containment. It concerns her relationship with Bob and Marco. As I have already mentioned, Bob embodies law and order (which in the end seems to mean unquestioned/unquestionable legitimated violence). Nikita, conversely, embodies feminine disruption (illegitimate violence outside patriarchal law). Bob, therefore, must not (but he clearly does) fall in love with her. To do so would be to experience the dissolution of his self (law and order) and his masculinity. He cannot embrace sexually that which challenges the very law, social order, he embodies. Thus he 'gets' to her through Marco – displaced fulfilment, sex by proxy – and also through imposing, for a second time, his 'rebirthing' of her: he packages her up for Marco by 'giving' her a past – displacement and containment, she is his fantasy. Bob can hide his desire behind this double displacement. Not so Nikita. Because she behaves transgressively in loving two men (Bob and Marco) she must disappear. And this is why. It is made clear that the attraction between Bob and Nikita is mutual but she also loves Marco. So instead of affirming the unified subjectivity of the male, Nikita as 'other' returns the image *of* and *to* man as a divided self – since it is not one reflection but two that she returns. Thus she once again shatters the discourses that the cultural construction of femininity are supposed to serve. By returning an image of doubleness, she constitutes a real threat to the ideological construction of gender, male gender, as unified and heterosexual. In this respect, Nikita becomes the source for male paranoia around his sexuality – she is acting in excess and so must go.

Conclusion

Spectator pleasure in a Besson film derives from the protagonists' ultimate ability to defy control; even to ridicule control (as in *Subway* and *Léon* where the forces of control are represented as ineffectual or corrupt). Spectator identification, also a source of pleasure, results from the recognisability of Besson's characters. Larger than life they may be (and why not if they are being imaged in scope), but they hook into desires and frustrations felt by audiences who have come to see, watch and empathise with narratives of lives that reflect their own. The technology, the environments, the social order of things – these are all systems and sites that remain hostile to a generation, the youth generation, that has to meet with sometimes insurmountable difficulties in order to become integrated. This is the world Besson portrays for his audiences and it is one they recognise. And this does endow him with a bardic function: he both reflects and exposes the post-industrial society in which we live, the society of post-industrial decay and commodity capitalism. In this respect he merits the label attached to him as a postmodern filmmaker. The term 'postmodern' requires a little explanation as does the way in which it can be ascribed to Besson. So let me explain this idea by way of conclusion. As you will see it will act as a springboard into the next chapter.

In order to be 'post' anything, there has to have been the moment in history that came before. Thus, by implication, if we are now living in the post-industrial society this means that we are no longer living in the industrial society. The industrial society was the moment of the industrial machine of the nineteenth-century Industrial Revolution, the society of *production* when industry served man as producer. The industrial era was the era of production. But we now live in the era of the post-industrial machine and the age of electronic media. It is instructive that we do not speak of a post-Industrial Revolution but that we can be said to live in the world of 'post-production'. What does this mean? This post-industrial society is one of *re*-production and recycling – one that no longer produces the real, but reproduces it. The goal of the post-industrial society, then, is to simulate the real. These two societies – the industrial and the post-industrial – are referred to respectively by cultural critics as the age of modernism and postmodernism.

Modernism finds its roots in the Enlightenment period of the eighteenth century and in man's (*sic*) belief in the power of human reasoning to understand the world. In this context, man is referred to as the transcendental subject. Modernism, as a concept, represented an optimistic belief in progress, in science and technology as man's tools whereby he could implement change. Modernism was also the time of the Industrial Revolution of the nineteenth century and was a logical outcome of the belief in man and technology (as a term 'technology' means discourses (logos) on the means of production or the science of industrial arts (technos)). This was the brave age of reinforced steel which enabled the construction of multi-storied buildings, railways, iron bridges, and so on. But this was also the era of mass-production, of factories and conveyor-belt work. It was an era of the industrial machine which led, in turn, to the alienation of the subject (the worker) who no longer commanded the modes of production. This then was the beginning of the age of modernism which stretched through until the mid-twentieth century at least.

Since the 1950s we have been living in a post-industrial era which has become increasingly one of post-industrial decay. It is this latter one in particular which Besson so faithfully records in his films, especially in *Le Dernier Combat*. But he even takes this recording so far as to reconstruct studio spaces ancient and modern within derelict and abandoned factories – as he did for *Nikita*. In this film, there is something so aptly postmodern about reconstructing, within the same disused Seita factories at Pantin, the set for the beautiful and baroque Train Bleu restaurant alongside the modern technological spaces of surveillance (the State Secret Service headquarters). This is truly artifice, post-production within post-industrial decay.

According to Fredric Jameson, we are post-everything: post-history, post-colonial, post-modern and so on.[58] Postmodernism is an eclectic term with both positive and negative connotations (similarly to modernism). On the positive side it is seen as a reaction against the extremes of modernism's belief in the benefits of science and technology to human kind. Positive is of course

58 Fredric Jameson 'Postmodernism and the Cultural Logic of Late Capitalism', *New Left Review*, no. 46, 1984, 53–93.

a nuanced term since this view of postmodernism is to see it as challenging the belief in human reason and disputing the cast-iron logic of structures and systems that modernism puts in place. Viewed in this reactive context, postmodern culture is one that is traumatised by a modernist technology that has created ideological structures of suppression and repression never seen before (the holocausts of World War Two: gas chambers and the Atom bomb to name but two).

On the more negative side, postmodernism is defined as coming after, as looking back, as lacking its own history (because it is defined only in relation to the past). Indeed, in its lack of history it rejects history and, because it has none of its own, stands eternally fixed in a series of presents. Viewed in this context, postmodern culture is non-oppositional and does not challenge what is past. Rather it can only *recycle* what is past. This idea of recycling is closely associated to the notion that post-industrialism recycles waste, that it needs its waste in order to live, that it recycles dead styles. It survives on dead styles and seeks only perfect simulation (as with Besson's set of the Train Bleu restaurant). It invents nothing. It pastiches culture. Baudrillard explains this pastiche culture in the following way: because this culture is reproducing what has already been reproduced, postmodern culture reproduces not the real (for that has already been produced) but the hyper-real, that is, a simulacrum of the real – perfect simulation.[59] Virtual reality is an extreme example of this hyper-real, and it is worth thinking that wars can now be fought or strategised pre-battle in virtual reality (as happened with the Gulf War).

Contemporary architecture can serve as an example of this recycling and perfect simulation. So many postmodern façades of buildings are a pastiche of Roman colonnades, Georgian windows and Victorian stained glass (all in one building). We no longer necessarily know to what original they might refer. Baudrillard would argue that that does not even matter since, in its obsession to perfect its simulation, postmodern culture no longer invokes

59 Jean Baudrillard (1983) *Simulations* (trans. Paul Foss, Paul Patton and Philip Beitchman), New York, Semiotext(e), 142–146.

the original as a point of comparison: the reproduction, the simulation is the point. Other illustrative examples can be found in the recording industry. Nowadays the dead can sing in harmony with the living. Thus, two singers who have never sung together in real life can be mixed together and packaged as the most natural combination of singers ever (as in the case of Nat King Cole and his daughter). Or, an earlier song can be recycled as a completely new one to the unsuspecting consumer. Thus, in Besson's *Subway*, a Johnny Nash song of the 1960s, 'I Can See Clearly Now', is reproduced as 'It's Only Mystery' and signed Eric Serra. This lack of invocation of the original as a point of comparison means that there is no distinction between the real and the copy. And it is in this loss of distinction between real and representation that Baudrillard perceives the death of the subject, the individual. If there is no distinction between real and simulacrum how can you signify as distinct? If you recycle dead styles how else can you signify except as lack, as death? You *re*-present nothing, you merely simulate it.

This idea of non-representation except as lack is particularly strong in Besson's film *Nikita*. But there is evidence of it in all his films, starting with *Le Dernier Combat*. I want to put in place one more piece of the postmodern jigsaw – concerning history – before referring back to Besson's work. Non-representation as lack is perceived as a by-product of the post-industrial machine. Whereas the industrial machine led to the alienation of the subject (through the lack of control of the means of production), the post-industrial machine, because it merely reproduces, goes one step further and leads to the fragmentation of the subject and its concomitant dispersal in representation. If it is fragmented, how can the subject represent its self to itself as a unity? In its fragmented state, the self shows all the signs of embodying a schizophrenic condition. The question becomes 'who am I'? Add to this the fact that, as we have just stated, within the negative view of postmodernism, the subject has no history, it is stuck in the ever present, so it is in effect without memory and the question again becomes, how can the subject represent its self to itself? According to Lacan, the experience of temporality (past, present, future, memory) and its representation are an effect of language. We use language to represent notions of temporality, and the idea of historical continuity.[60] If, however, the subject has no experience of temporality, no links with the past (lacking history), then it is without language. That is, it lacks the means of representing the 'I'. This again creates a schizophrenic condition in which, this time, the subject fails to assert its subjectivity in language (because it cannot 'speak'). The subject fails, therefore, to enter the Symbolic Order (the social order of things, patriarchal order). The subject remains stuck in the Imaginary Order (the pre-linguistic moment). And the question becomes not just 'who am I', but 'who made me'? In other words, where is the mother?

As far as film is concerned, it is instructive that the past ten years or so have witnessed a spate of monster films and that central to their narrative has been the question of reproduction and identity. If we just take as recent examples *Jurassic Park* (Spielberg, 1993), *Mary Shelley's Frankenstein* (Branagh, 1994) and *Interview with the Vampire* (Jordan, 1994), an analysis of these films reveals that the missing link between the past, present and the future is the figure of the mother. She is absent from these films as the site of reproduction. Instead *the* reproduction machine of post-industrialism, male technology, has reproduced 'her' through genetic engineering. The original is not even referred to: genetic engineering replaces the womb, 'perfectly' simulating the idea of reproduction. Dinosaurs, monsters, vampires – cyborgs of our worst imaginings – these are the creatures of the age of simulacrum (to which we can now add the very hyper-real Dolly, the first cloned sheep). These films express repressed fears around technology, of course. But they also express fears about being born into lack and as having no identity. Besson's films, whilst less extreme perhaps, also express these concerns. Why otherwise do his characters speak so little or not at all? The main

60 For a very helpful reading of Lacan's notion of temporality, schizophrenia and the postmodern, see Giuliana Bruno's wonderful essay on *Blade Runner*: 'Ramble City: Postmodernism and *Blade Runner*', *October*, vol. 41, 1987, 61–74. I am indebted to her analysis in this section on the fragmented post-industrial subject.

protagonists are almost without language. The protagonist of *Le Dernier Combat* cannot speak (bar one moment with the doctor), Fred almost had his vocal chords severed forever and cannot sing, Jacques can only communicate soundlessly with dolphins, Nikita is virtually without language and Léon is similarly inarticulate. Except for Jacques, none of Besson's characters have a history and the only histories told are pure fiction, as in the case of Nikita who has no history of her own but has it narrated for her by Bob. Jacques' history is about the loss of the father. Nikita has no mother, nor does Mathilda. Parents abound by their absence in Besson's movies, particularly the mother. This singular absence of parents in Besson's films points to the death of the family. Indeed, when they are present in a film, usually as 'proto-parents' (another simulacrum), they are as dysfunctional as the adult-child they purport to parent. They are no more than crippled cyphers passing on the same institutionalised messages of which they were themselves 'victim' (recycling).

In this chapter, we have examined the regressive and transgressive disposition of Besson's protagonists – particularly in relation to technology. We have discussed their refusal to enter the social order of things and shown that their revolt is perhaps a source of spectator pleasure. But the question remains, why do Besson's protagonists appear from nowhere only to find oblivion? One reading would be that these are 'children' of a post-industrial age who have no means, except through their oblivion (aesthetically achieved), to mark and represent their lack, their non-identity. Their oblivion, through the body disappearing, makes their absence presence at the very moment of disappearance. An embodied spectacle of lack. The next chapter will pick up on this point and seek to develop it further within the context of the dysfunctional/absent family.

What of this post-industrial child and the world in which it lives? The morally bankrupt world that Besson's films reflect is completely contemporaneous with the Mitterrand era (1981–95) – an era which promised everything to a new generation (even to the point of inventing a slogan, *la génération Mitterrand*, and slapping it on to an electoral poster with a baby on it). And yet it is an era which failed to provide hope and future security for the youth generation and one that has indeed been implicated in numerous financial scandals and dubious suicides. In the next chapter we will examine Besson's films in the context of this death of the family and the socio-political climate of the times and suggest ways in which Besson fights back against the unbalancing effects of contemporary society on the family and, thereby, the youth generation for whom he seems to speak.

4

Constructing subjectivity in the absence of the father and mother

One cannot fail to notice the regressive nature in Besson's films of all of his central protagonists. Characters retreat into a child-like-ness and from there often encounter death. Thus, Héléna in *Subway* erupts like a petulant teenager, Fred persists in his childhood fantasy to produce a rock-band. Jacques in *Le Grand Bleu* returns to the preter-human state of a dolphin (in his mind at least). The eponymous protagonists Nikita and Léon remain woman-child and man-child respectively. Nor do any of these children of Besson seem over-anxious to live a long life. Jacques and Léon essentially commit suicide; Fred gets killed and Nikita disappears off the face of the earth. We are here encountering a reiteration of the death of the subject rather than any seeming construction of subjectivity. It is instructive also in relation to this question of subjectivity that the mother and father – the two psychological necessities to one's sense of identity (according to Freud and Lacan) – are singularly not there, particularly the mother. No one can fail to notice the absence of the family. How their absence is marked is equally significant. In *Le Dernier Combat* and *Subway* there is no family – complete erasure – there is only the presence of the patriarchal figure in the form of the doctor in the former film and the police and jealous husband in the latter. In *Le Grand Bleu* the father drowns; in *Nikita* the mother is a non-being (an absence invoked). In *Léon* the family is decimated. Surrogate or 'proto'-parents, on the rare occasions that they are represented or are present, are no solution since they are as dysfunctional as the adult-child they are purporting to parent. One thinks of Uncle Louis in *Le Grand Bleu* and of course, differently but still dysfunctional, the eponymous hero of *Léon*.

The question, then, becomes twofold. Why this regressiveness and why this absence of the family? We know from Besson's own words that he is consternated by the dissolution of the family in contemporary French society, so clearly its absence in his films is not a transparent and innocent absence. The family is absent for a reason. This chapter is going to investigate these issues of transgressive 'child' and absent parent in Besson's films and is going to do so through the triple-optic of genre and gender construction, regression and pathology, resistance and power relations. Although all three frameworking optics overlap, I shall – as with previous chapters – be using separate headings for this tripartite investigation.

Genre and gender construction

Let us first of all consider the genres that Besson's films exemplify. It is noteworthy that in the main his films are hybrid genres. Thus *Subway* is a musical and a thriller. *Léon* is a thriller and a melodrama. *Nikita* is a *film noir* and a futurist fantasy. Only *Le Dernier Combat* and *Le Grand Bleu* appear to be single generic types. The former is a sci-fi film and the latter an adventure film. Mixing genres is not a new phenomenon in French cinema, the French New Wave of the early 1960s was just one moment in its film history where genre-hybridisation was massively practised. But what interests us here are the kind of genres Besson has chosen to hybridise and what they tell us in a first instance about gender construction.

Sci-fi and adventure films are traditionally gendered as masculine: the subject-matter is identified as masculine because most often the central protagonists are male and of course because science is seen as a marker of man's rationality, his power to understand the world. Adventure movies are also traditionally gendered as masculine. The implication then is that women will be quite marginal in these types of films, and indeed *Le Dernier Combat* and *Le Grand Bleu* precisely replicate this marginality of woman and centrality of the male. As far as these genres are concerned, typically, in the adventure film the male is full of action and in the sci-fi movie full of rationality (at least at the beginning). The narrative challenges man's capacity for action and quick thinking but in the end he wins out. In Besson's films this winning-out closure is highly ambiguous. Masculinity does not assert itself very assuredly in *Le Dernier Combat*. The protagonist may have won the battle but one feels the war is already lost. He may get the woman, but to what avail? The sci-fi nightmare is close to coming true: man has destroyed himself through the very technology that he invented to win his wars. There is no hint of order (that is, man's rationality) being restored. Masculinity is equally unsafe in *Le Grand Bleu*. Here the adventure is to defy life and actively seek death – a reverse of the action-packed adventure movie conventions we are accustomed to where the action-hero comes up trumps. In this reversal of conventions – in that Jacques goes down drowning – there is something rather feminising in his disappearance and death, hand on fin, with a dolphin. Masculinity avails but to no avail. Man, in these two Besson films, experiences the limits of liminality rather than the triumph of universal rationality.

The hybrid films produce – through their generic counter-pointing – similarly intriguing constructions of gender. And I will examine how this functions in Besson's work by focusing on just two of his films, *Subway* and *Léon*. *Subway* is a mixture of musical and thriller. The musical, a typically Hollywood genre, traditionally narrates the boy meets girl scenario: boy meets girl, boy does not like girl, boy gradually grows to like girl and eventually loves girl and they marry. In other words the musical (a Hollywood genre *par excellence*) sells marriage. It works to reconcile the differences between the two sexes and, in the closing sequence, the triumphant formation of the couple metaphorically serves as a redemption of society itself as a utopian collectivity, the community as a social ideal. Conversely, the thriller is about suspense, retribution and death: how, why, when will the protagonist get caught and killed?

The mood is one of fear and apprehension, paranoia even. The protagonist is the one pursued through labyrinthine streets and sewers of the city, constantly aware that she or he is under surveillance. Thus, to mix these two genres is like matching utopia (musical = marriage) with dystopia (thriller = threat of death). As a genre, the thriller's closure serves to explain the death of the subject and so leaves the spectator with a meaningful death (thus preserving the notion of a unified subject). The musical's closure serves to assert the subject as a signifying presence in the heterosexual imperative. The effect of the hybridisation of these two genres in *Subway* in terms of narrative closure is one of clashing: the musical meets its death in the Paris métro – one closure ironises the other. And this is perhaps the real meaning of Fred's apparent rising from the dead and laughing in the final frame. In the end we are not sure if he is indeed dead, so we are uncertain as to what we have in fact witnessed. We witness redemption and loss in one set of images (Héléna's declaration of love to the dying Fred); but we also witness absence, as represented through the death of the subject, being denied at the final frame. Narrative closure is thus both foregrounded and questioned. The tragic ending, Héléna at last confesses her love for Fred and he dies, meets comic relief, Fred lifts his head and grins from ear to ear. This clashing of closures defies the traditional satisfactory ending of these generic films which offers either the heterosexual couple (marriage in the musical) or the notion of a unified subject (meaningful death in the thriller). We get both endings in Besson's film, but in that they clash we get neither. The heterosexual imperative is emptied of meaning as is death itself. Death is not meaningful, it may even be a fake: Fred does not necessarily die. In any event, death as retribution is in excess of Fred's actions, there is no real motivation behind his erasure, so again his death has no meaning and does not 'explain' Fred to us as 'a man who had to die'. So the notion of a unified subject is lost and without meaning. Similarly, the myths of romantic love, heroism and destiny – tropes of popular cinema – are emptied out and shown as inadequate in the oxymoronic and excessive closure(s) to *Subway*.

What then does this play with genre tell us about gender construction? If the unified subject and the heterosexual imperative are not assured by the narrative closure of *Subway* then it is obvious that gender fixity is just as unstable. This instability is also marked in this film through the play with dress-codes and various forms of cross-dressing.

Let us start with the concept of the unified subject. According to Freud and, later, Lacan, subjectivity (identity) is based in the notion of difference – sexual difference. With regard to subjectivity, child development goes through three essential phases. First, the child has an imaginary sense of unity with the mother through the breast. Second, the child goes through what is called the mirror stage and, finally, it enters the Oedipal phase. In the second so-called mirror phase, the mother holds the child up to the mirror. The child now imagines an illusory, imaginary identification with its self reflected in the mirror (the part of the mirror stage known as narcissism). It perceives itself as a unified being, as one and the same with the reflection. However, it quickly recognises that this identification is illusory. It is not a unified subject even at the simplest of levels because it cannot take control of its bodily movements, it depends on the mother to hold it up to the mirror. It is at this point that the child perceives its difference or sameness with the mother. Simultaneously, the child senses the loss/absence of the mother (the loss of the breast, and the ensuing loss of a sense of unity with her).

It is at this stage in the mirror phase that sexual difference enters into play for the male child. The male child perceives that he is sexually different from his mother: that he has a penis and she does not. Her lack is constructed as absence to his phallic presence – her absence confirms his presence, she is his structuring absence. But the male child, in perceiving the mother as lacking a penis, is also filled with the fear of castration. The mother represents what he could lose. So she becomes potentially the castrating mother – the one who could deny his sexual identity by removing his difference. However, this first recognition of sexual identity through difference is also marked by the need for the presence of the mother, the female 'other', to secure the sense of self as subject (his difference, his subjectivity which she asserted in the mirror phase). This then brings the child to the third stage of sexual development: the Oedipal complex. The child, sensing his difference from his mother, but still desiring unification with her to assert his identity, now wishes to bond sexually with her. His father intercedes and prohibits the incestual drive and the child must now seek to bond with a female who is not his mother (the female other). If he disobeys, the punishment he risks is castration, this time by the father.

Castration then is the threat to male subjectivity, it is the end of difference, it signifies as lack and as meaninglessness. Castration represents the subject's own death. The female (m)other and the father both threaten the male subject with annihilation, non-subjectivity. At the end of *Subway*, Fred is caught in the crossfire (literally) of the female gaze (Héléna looking at him as she runs towards him) and the phallic symbol of patriarchal power (the gun that shoots him dead). But Héléna is 'cross-dressed' as masculine, she is wearing a man's grey suit and Fred has foresaken his dinner suit for a girl's sweater, buttoned at the back, and a poorly fitting macintosh. Dress-codes are far from secure here. Similarly Fred's own death is far from stable: he dies laughing and laughs at his dying – so where is the castrating fear of death?

The thriller, *film noir*, gangster film are all generic types that play out man's pathological fear of castration and death. They are genres that allow man to represent death to himself, to contain it and thereby tame it even though, as we know, it is impossible to represent our own death to ourselves. These genres fulfil a double function then: they remind man of what happens if he does not follow patriarchal law and enter the social order of things by reproducing patriarchy (refusal to obey the law of the father will bring about the death of patriarchy) and it also provides a means of imaging his worst fantasy, his own death. The musical, conversely, allows heterosexuality to signify its purpose to itself: reproduction of the self – life itself. Besson, in counterpointing the generic type of the thriller with that of the musical, suggests the very instability of what these two genres seek to represent to the spectator: the crucial importance of sexual difference and the heterosexual imperative. And if generic representation is so unstable then so too must be gender representation. Why and how is this so?

Gender has a socio-cultural origin that is ideological in purpose and which seeks to fuse the notions of biological sex and sexuality and represent them as one and the same (that is, gender = sex = sexuality). Thus, the ideological function of gender is to fix us as either male or female and this is the first in a set of binary oppositions that serve to fix us as such. These binary oppositions are socially, psychologically, physically and biologically grounded. So the female is economically inferior to the male, is associated more with the domestic sphere than the public sphere, is more emotional, less strong than the male. She is the site of reproduc-tion (at least for the time being, though the 'progress' on cloning will soon eliminate that, one presumes). She is not the site of production which is the male domain, and so on. It is clear how this essentialist approach (woman is this/man is that) fixes gender and leads to a naturalising of gender difference (we accept it as 'natural'). However, gender is not a simple case of sexual difference as ideology would have us believe, but a series of hierarchical power relations cleverly disguised so as to hide the way in which gender is imposed by force. Cultural practices (such as cinema, television, advertising) reproduce gender ideology often at the expense of other forms of social determination such as class, race and sexuality. And the question is of course why? Psychoanalysis, or rather the strong investment in psychoanalytic discourses is a pathway to finding the answer. Whilst psycho-analysis may well expose the social order of things as determined by patriarchal law, it does nothing in reality to counter it. In a sense it sanctions patriarchal law, that is dominant western ideology. Within the triangular formation of the family, we learn that the law of the father is the one that must be obeyed. The myth of Oedipus conveniently lives on – at least in its abridged form.

By reducing subjectivity to a fixed gendered entity (as masculine or feminine), dominant ideology (patriarchy) normalises away questions of power relations. And yet it is clear that power relations affect gender relations. In the western world, we live not only in a patriarchal world but also a homosocial one. Power is invested in the masculine and, in order for it to stay there, men bond (the political and economic establishment, military forces, just to name two obvious instances). Racial and class difference are other categories that gender ideology seeks to dissimulate. Why otherwise the prurience with the sexual potency of the black male or the working-class man? They are perceived first as their sex: the potent phallus. This fixing of a gendered subjectivity (which excludes the notion of a multiple one) attempts to disguise the fact that gender is not as stable as ideology would have us believe. And yet gender ideology is inscribed into just so many cultural practices that surround us daily. Indeed, it is worth recalling that Hollywood is obsessed with selling gender difference and heterosexuality. The question becomes, where in gender ideology does one situate cross-dressing, transvestism, trans-sexualism, homosexuality? The answer is, one does not. These sexualities that do not fit get erased as difference and defined in terms of otherness – or as sexually deviant (as marginalised outside the notion of sexual difference).

This is where Besson's play with dress-codes and cross-dressing starts to have more than just a surface meaning. Cross-dressing foregrounds the performance aspect of dress: we are gender-coded by our dress. So cross-dressing problematises gender identity and sexual identity: 'change your clothes and change your sex'.[1] Cross-dressing plays with the distance between the outer-clothed self and the self underneath. Thus sexual disguise plays on gender fixity, makes it possible to think about it as fluid. With its potential to denaturalise sexual difference (denaturalise ideology's naturalising of gender difference) and thereby threaten ideological fixity, it is unsurprising that cross-dressing in mainstream cinema is quite safely contained. In other words we are never duped as to the 'true' sexual identity beneath

1 For more detailed discussion of cross-dressing, see Annette Kuhn's (1985) brilliant essay 'Sexual Disguise and Cinema', in A. Kuhn, *The Power of the Image: Essays on Representation and Sexuality*, London and New York, Routledge & Kegan Paul.

the suit or dress. We know if the phallus is there or not. And it is probably because of its potential to threaten that for the most part cross-dressing in mainstream cinema occurs in comedies or musicals where, given the nature of these genres as relatively asexual and unrealistic, it functions as a source of laughter.

Cross-dressing in Besson's film *Subway* is not, however, located within a single genre so what happens when, as with this film, it occurs across two genres – thriller and musical? Where is it located in that film at any time? If it is within the musical then it is presumably safe and contained, if the thriller then presumably unsafe and uncontained. Héléna in disguising her female-gendered body through male-gendered clothing crosses the gender boundaries as easily as she crosses genre boundaries and exposes both sets of boundaries as unstable. The price of such exposure, however, is high. In mainstream cinema, women who successfully cross gender boundaries are punished for their transgressiveness. Besson's film is no exception to this. In Héléna's case, she loses the man she loves and is by all appearances recaptured by her husband's hit-men. A similar punishment is meted out to Nikita in Besson's film of that same name. The price she pays for her initially successful masquerading as male and gaining access to secret files is to be unmasked as a fake and consigned to oblivion. The ideological message is clear: women who make their structuring absence presence and who thereby denaturalise gender ideology are not to be countenanced and must be forced back into absence. If a woman cross-dresses successfully as male she is not just disguising her sexuality, she is masquerading as phallic. She purports to possess the very thing she cannot possess, and *unless* she suppresses desire (which makes her disguise safe) she becomes the embodiment of the very otherness that gender ideology cannot tolerate. In her actively agencing desire for the male as cross-dressed, s/he embodies homosexual desire. In other words, her cross-dressing exposes the very thing gender ideology seeks to conceal: the fact that we live in a homosocial environment. If successful, the cross-dressed woman blatantly posits the question of the relationship between homo-socialism and homoeroticism – the very question that patriarchal law obliges man to suppress into his unconscious.[2]

The argument is not necessarily that Besson deliberately sets out to expose these ideological practices of gender construction, but to suggest that through hybridising genres he has brought about that effect. Even the non-hybridised films raise questions around gender ideology. If we think about *Le Grand Bleu* and the form that male-bonding takes in that film we can see that homosociality is based not in power relations but in brotherly love. Male-bonding here leads to death – a form of narcissistic homo-eroticism – not to the fulfilment of patriarchal law. One has to wonder therefore if somewhere in all of this Besson is not positing a lack of desire for the patriarch. Certainly an analysis of the generic and generic foregrounding in *Léon* would seem to confirm this reading.

Léon is a family melodrama without the family and a thriller whose excess has no pretence to realism. Family melodramas, which developed alongside nineteenth-century capitalism, are traditionally gendered as feminine, primarily because they are located in the home or domestic sphere. We must bear in mind that the family is the site of patriarchy and privatised capitalism (nineteenth-century capitalism gave rise to the need for the family to protect, through the inheritance system, the bourgeoisie's wealth), so there is the potential for conflict within the family environment between the male sphere of capital production and the female domestic sphere of reproduction. The genre serves to make sense of the family and in so doing perpetuates it, including

2 Geoffrey Brown in his article 'Gender and the Action Heroine: *Hardbodies* and the *Point of no Return*', *Cinema Journal*, vol. 35, no. 3, 1996, argues for another reading of play with gender in *Nikita*. He argues, mistakenly to my mind, that there is little difference between Besson's film *Nikita* and the American remake *Point of no Return* and suggests that Maggie/Nikita's 'masculinity is disguised by her feminine masquerade' (67). He goes on to say that it is in this way that the 'artificiality of both masculine and feminine roles is exposed' (*ibid.*). Perhaps within the American version this is true. However, this argument does not stand up so well in the case of Besson's film. Nikita struggles against gender fixity but she constantly has gender fixity imposed upon her. She is dressed as phallic for her first mission, she is a maid-servant on her second, she is woman-child on her third, finally she is cross-dressed as male but exposed as a fraud on her final mission.

the continuation of the subordination of woman and the suppression of her agencing desire. However, there is a twist. Because the male finds himself in the domestic sphere, he is no longer in the site of production but of reproduction. Thus the home represents the potential site for the confrontation between production and reproduction. And a resolution cannot be brought about without compromise. And the male – who finds himself in the female, non-active, even passive, sphere – has to function on terms that are appropriate to the domestic sphere: he has to see the value of domestic life for if he does not only violence and turbulence will prevail. For the family to survive a compromise has to be reached, the male has to become less male and in the process he becomes more feminised. What must be suppressed at all costs are inadmissible desire and violence so that the image of the triangular family remains safe. The effect of this compromise is one of repressed desire (sexual desire for the female which she cannot agence, castration fear for the male who fears his feminisation).

The melodrama is, then, about generational and gender conflict and repressed desire, all of which get played out in the claustrophobic environs of the domestic sphere. The mood is often one of paranoia because the family feels under threat and thus so too does patriarchy. The thriller is also imbued with paranoia, but this time not so much in the domestic sphere as out in the city streets. As we have already stated, it is a genre that is identified as masculine and one which plays out man's pathological fear of castration and death. Thus, with *Léon*, by hybridising the feminine genre with the masculine, Besson produces, once again, a generic clashing or indeed deliberate 'confusion' of genres. The masculine of the thriller confounds the feminine of the melodrama; the one genre pulls against the other, creating a sense of confusion in an environment of claustrophobia and paranoia where one genre struggles with the issue of compromise between the sexes and the other runs in fear of its masculine life. I think this notion of confusion is helpful in relation to *Léon* because it enables us to examine gender roles under a similar light, as confusion. The interplay between these two genres allows Besson to come at questions of gender construction and its representation in a slightly different way from his previous films. Gender fixity is still in question but not in the same motivated way that it was in Besson's *Subway* and *Nikita*. In other words, the confusion around gender emanates from the characters themselves – the inner confusion gets exteriorised and displayed *through* rather than *on* the body.

In the context of Besson's bringing two genres together it is easy to see that melodrama is linked to the thriller at least through the notion of the repressed and its concomitant manifestation, paranoia. When I say that *Léon* is a family melodrama without the family, I mean to say that the actual and real family, Mathilda's family that is, gets removed right at the beginning of the film. From the brief scenes that we see of her family life we quickly understand that clashes, conflicts and ruptures are a constant. There seems no respite from this incessant explosion of family tension whether it be in the form of the dysfunctional father who beats his children or the passively available step-mother who treats 'her' children with little more than dismissive contempt. It is no mistake that Mathilda comes across the parental couple copulating. The primal scene is not usually given visible space in melodrama, but it is very much a structuring absence – we sense it is always lurking just behind in the shadows. In *Léon*, there is no attempt at compromise on the part of the father, so the domestic sphere becomes one where the inner violence (an effect of repression) explodes outwardly – hence the visibilisation of the copulating parents. To experience the primal scene is to witness sex as a form of violence visited by the father upon the mother. It is perceived by the child as a threat to the family unity and is closely associated with death. In *Léon*, this visibilisation has meta-phoric value: instead of resolving conflicts, the father exacerbates them through his violent behaviour.[3] Mathilda for her part displaces the sense of alienation and oppression she feels within the family in a number of ways. A first form of her displaced behaviour is self-damaging, turning her alienation in on herself. Thus, she smokes. More importantly still, she plays hookie from

3 We note also that violence finally erupts fully in the form of the massacre perpetrated by Stansfield.

school, and she takes that absence further still to the point of announcing over the telephone to the headmistress, enquiring as to her whereabouts, that she is dead. A mythic self-erasure maybe but a verbalisation of a wish-fulfilment that is directly related to her family environment. The second form of her displaced behaviour is one of substitution. She becomes the surrogate mother to her baby brother, the only person for whom she feels any love. In this respect we could argue that she steps into the gap and makes up for the parents' dysfunctionality. This is a role which she is doomed to fail to fulfil not just because her brother gets killed in the massacre but because displacement by substitution cannot cover over the cracks that the dysfunctional family opens up. Finally, within the logic of melodrama, Mathilda is doomed to fail because she cannot occupy a position that is not 'rightfully' hers (to say nothing of the fact that as a 12-year-old it would be biologically impossible for her to have a 4-year-old son).

Failure notwithstanding, this is the role she has adopted at the beginning of the film's narrative. And as we shall see, it is one she never fully relinquishes. By taking away her role as 'mother' through the brutal killing of her 'son' she loses all claim to family. Her anger and desire for revenge for this obliteration produces a fragmentation of or shift in her ideologically gendered role as female and she goes on to occupy a multiplicity of positions in relation to gender and sexuality. This process begins when she goes to Léon for refuge, which he eventually provides for her. In a sequence previous to the massacre, Léon had shown kindness towards her when she was sitting crying and smoking on the landing. He tells her to stop smoking and offers her a handkerchief. It is that kindness that she relies upon to persuade him to let her into his room when her life is in danger. From that moment on their relationship, arguably as viewed from Mathilda's eyes, shifts. Léon becomes the father she never had, the brother she lost and, finally more troublingly, the male other whom she desires. As for Mathilda, she occupies, in turn, the position of daughter, mother, lover. However, each one of these positions is touched by paradox in that Mathilda appears to occupy both sides of the gender divide, producing the fragmentation mentioned above. Let us explore this further.

As daughter she mostly obeys Léon. However, she commands him to teach her his hit-man skills. She accepts his discipline around her training-up to be a hit-woman, but she has the means to pay him to train her up so the exchange has parity. But what strikes of course is that she is doubly occupying a male role. First, as a trained killer manipulating phallic technology of death, she occupies a position more traditionally associated with the male; second, as economically independent and a commander of capital, she has the power to pay for what she wants and she occupies, therefore, a space in the market place of exchange that is equal to man's; her purchasing power enables her to buy Léon's services in much the same way as Tony (his Mafia contract boss). This potential subversion of gender fixity gets recouped, however, into her position as female as the following explanation of her second position as mother makes clear. As mother she nurtures Léon (she gets the milk) and teaches him to read and write. Yet again we face a possible inversion of power, with Léon as the infantilised son and Mathilda as the all-knowing mother. But this is short-lived and parity is apparently restored. Thanks to the transference of skills, Léon is able to find Mathilda and rescue her when her life is at risk (he reads the note she has left him before she goes off on her mission to kill Stansfield). Although one could read their mutual exchanging of skills as a form of parity, there is a problem here nonetheless. Léon teaches Mathilda how to shoot, but she does not yet know how to mount a kill. So she is inept when she sets off on her mission to remove Stansfield; Léon, conversely, knows not only how to read (and understand the note), he also knows how to enter a building, remove a target and rescue Mathilda. The exchange of skills is not then one of parity so, by implication, she is returned to her former roles of daughter and mother. Finally, as lover, once more the chain of signification is fraught. Misrecognition, transference and substitution are all at work here. Mathilda transfers her love of her brother on to Léon, so he becomes the substitute loved one for her and in so doing she misrecognises him as the object of her desire. Instead of transferring her love of her father on to Léon, which is (in psychoanalysis) the 'normal' route to entry into the social order of things and maturity, it is her love of her brother that gets transferred. But the father and transference is not far away. We know that Mathilda hates her father; thus, in Léon she finds a father substitute. By wishing to become Léon's lover we could argue that she is going through the female Oedipal phase that she never underwent with her real father. However, as Freudian analysis tells us, this is to misrecognise the object of one's desire and the (female) child must transfer that love on to a male other. What we are suggesting, therefore, is that Mathilda is caught doubly-desiring and that both forms of desiring are ultimately 'proto'-incestuous (loving the substitute brother and father). What we can also suggest is that, having lost one family, she is desperately trying to re-create another, this time on her terms but with a limited number of people available. Hence the shifting roles that she and ultimately Léon are obliged to adopt. However, such a fragmentation of the subject leads as we know to its dispersal in representation. In its fragmented state the subject shows all the signs of embodying a schizophrenic condition. And the question is: 'who am I?'.

Léon plays father, son and lover. But he assumes that latter role only when it is too late. Or, put another way, since the social order of things prohibits him from becoming Mathilda's lover, he gives up his body for her. He sacrifices the material body for the corporeal love that cannot be had. Equally significantly he pulls the plug (the pin of the hand grenade) on his life in exchange for that of Mathilda's. Having acknowledged his love for Mathilda, the only way that love can be sublimated is through death, that is, through a de-phallicising of the masculine body. This notion of the de-phallicised masculine body is in fact a trope of film melodrama. The phallus is made safe so that the social order of things remains safe and so that the family does not come under threat. A classic example of this melodramatic trope can be found in Douglas Sirk's *All that Heaven Allows* (1955). In this film, a middle-class widowed mother falls in love with her younger male employee, a gardener. She lives in middle-town America, the environment of stifling respectability (including that of her own college-age kids). Her world is one of sexual repression and (of course) obsession. In falling in love with her gardener she reaps the opprobrium of her children and the community at large. She renounces her love for the gardener, but by a twist of fortune at the end of the film she is allowed to 'reunite' with him. However, this re-unison with him is rendered totally safe because he has been rendered impotent (and bed-ridden) by a road accident. For fantasising too far, she only gets half her man. There will be no cross-age, cross-class fornication here.

We know that Besson denies that there is anything sexual about the love between Mathilda and Léon, but the point remains that Mathilda fantasises sexual union – even if it stays at the level of fantasy. It is surely not a pure coincidence that in this film and in *Nikita* there is an older father figure with whom the young female protagonists fall in love. The older man/younger woman Lolita-narrative is one that stretches far back into French film history, to the 1920s, and has its roots in a number of factors. The first is a historical one and has to do with the loss of life in the First World War. As a result of the 13 million Frenchmen who perished in that war, France was left without a male youth generation. The young women were more or less obliged therefore to marry older men (and French cinema had a role to play in the normalising of this social and demographic obligation). This master-narrative of French cinema prevailed through until the late 1950s only to reappear in the 1980s.[4] The reason for this resurgence of the father–daughter narrative in the 1980s can be surmised as a backlash phenomenon against the socio-economic progression of the status of women since the 1970s. But it can also be read as a response to the political cultural climate of the times of the 1980s during which there was a feeling of a loss of the patriarch in the form of the increasing ineffectuality and unpopularity of François Mitterrand, the man who had sold himself to the French electorate as (amongst other things) the patriarchal-president of France. In other words, the return of this master-narrative can be

4 For more detail on the father–daughter narrative, see Ginette Vincendeau's article in *Sight and Sound*, March 1992, 14–17.

seen as an attempt to substitute for what is not really there.[5]

Besson's play with this master-narrative clearly evolves from *Nikita* to *Léon*. In *Nikita*, the heroine is reduced to a child-woman state, she is infantilised and humiliated by the patriarch Bob. And yet we are left in no doubt that she has fallen in love with him, and he with her. Indeed his power over her is so great that her only recourse is to disappear completely, to be no longer visible to him as an object of desire. To stay within his gaze and power will mean eventually that she must get killed on one of his impossible missions that he orders her to undertake. To break the sadistic relationship (his power over her) she has to elect absence (an avowal of her powerlessness of course). In *Léon*, the father–daughter narrative is far more complex because Léon's own sexuality as we have already hinted is far from fixed and, as we have seen, the power relations constantly shift. Furthermore, Mathilda suffers no humiliation from the substitute father. Léon, as we argued in the previous chapter, embodies a feminised phallus and is not the phallic itself. We also argued that his infantilisation, whilst it constructs him as asexual, is a form of feminisation as well. We can add that Léon is not quick to reason, a so-called male attribute. Where he is quick is in the realm of the physical, the instinctual. To Mathilda's cognitive state corresponds Léon's physical one – suggesting a reversal of the animus/anima stereotypes, man as intellect/Logos, woman as bodily instinct/Eros. Over the course of the film, Mathilda's cognitive side develops to encompass the physical, and Léon's does likewise in the opposite direction. The earlier inner–outer match between the two characters (her animus to his anima) now becomes embodied by both. Let me explain what I believe is going on here.

According to Jung, in the unconscious of every man there is hidden a feminine personality (the anima, an unconscious feminine figure), a fact of which man is generally quite unaware; and in that of every woman a masculine personality (the animus). This figure often appears in dreams, visions, fantasies, emotions,

---

5 There are strong parallels here with the situation in France in the 1930s when political instability was rife and France lacked any sense of true leadership.

grotesque ideas and so on – but at the level of the unconscious.[6] Man (*sic*) for the most part suppresses any knowledge of an unconscious personality just as he suppresses his fear of sex and castration. According to Jung, however, these figures of the unconscious personality irrupt 'autonomously into consciousness as soon as it gets into a pathological state'.[7] The western world is inclined to 'swallow up the unconscious' or to suppress it.[8] We would now be inclined to add that it is in the interests of a patriarchal/homosocial world to pretend it does not exist. Jung goes on to point out the dangers of such suppression and such attempts at disavowal. If the conscious and the unconscious are not allowed to make a whole then the one ends up injuring the other. As Jung says: 'it is dangerous to suppress (the unconscious), because the unconscious is life and this life turns against us if suppressed, as happens in neurosis'.[9] The irruption of the unconscious personality into consciousness often amounts to a psychosis which Jung believes is a central effect of schizophrenia.[10]

Unlike Freud, who believed that schizophrenia was due to sexual repression and the withdrawal of erotic interest in the outside world in favour of an internalising of that interest, Jung 'believed that the loss of contact with reality characteristic of schizophrenia could not be attributed to sexual withdrawal alone'.[11] Jung believed the cause was not singular but complex and more likely to be psychological than physical in origin and so he came to use the term 'libido' to refer to psychic energy in general rather than limiting it to sexuality.[12] Jung believed, and here we can bear the character of Léon in mind, that when the 'natural course of a man's development through life was held up, either by

6 See C. G. Jung (1986) *Jung: Selected Writings* (selected and introduced by Anthony Storr), Hammersmith, Fontana Press. Where this unconscious feminine figure and other personifications of the unconscious personality find representation in the conscious world is in works of literature, mythology, religion and the visual arts.

7 *Ibid.*, 224.

8 *Ibid.*, 225.

9 *Ibid.*

10 *Ibid.*, 224.

11 Anthony Storr, *ibid.* (1986), 17.

12 *Ibid.*, 18.

misfortune or by his failure to face life's obligations, his libido became turned in on himself and reactivated the attitudes and feelings of childhood which would normally have been left behind him'.[13]

With the female, the animus is personified as male; with the male, the anima is personified as female. We know that Léon had an unhappy adventure with a woman and it is Tony who warns him to be careful not to get involved with women again (and Tony is referring to Léon's attachment to Mathilda). The inference is that he has been traumatised by this event and shut himself off from his emotions, cut off his female anima. In any event, we have plenty of evidence also that he has (re)activated the attitudes of childhood – or has always already embodied them. He is then both the hard man *and* the child who has turned his libido in on himself. The outer shell (the animus) does a massive cover-up job (through the pyrotechnic displays of his killing body) in its attempts to repress the anima. However, his regressive nature is there for all to see (clothing, analphabetism, asexuality, feminisation) and is in direct contradiction with the outer shell. This suggests that his consciousness has reached a pathological state – hence the obsession with the plant; hence too the obsessive and repetitive manipulation of his killing technology: 'kill and clean, kill and clean'; hence finally his autistic relationship with the outside world. Léon's unconscious, disavowed and distressed inner personality, the unconscious feminine figure, is close to irrupting into his consciousness, if it is not already there, producing the psychosis of schizophrenia.

By introducing Mathilda into Léon's life, Besson's stated aim was to get at the man behind the cold-blooded killer and show that beneath it all was a sensitive human being who was himself a victim. In order to bring this out, Besson had to find a means of getting him to speak. And the mechanism he used was Mathilda, 'une enfant, petite femme, fragile, innocente, dépendante, intelligente, tout ce qu'il n'est pas'.[14] To break the man of granite,

13 *Ibid.*
14 Besson (1995) 15, 'a little girl, a little woman, fragile, innocent, dependent, intelligent, everything he is not'.

Besson tells us, he uses the most fragile of flowers. In their relationship he perceives a perfect geometric structure. They are, he assures us 'si loin, si différents et en même temps si semblables et si proches. Désireux du même amour.'[15] The idea all along was that they would reflect one to the other so that in the end their repressed personalities would come forward to join in equal visibility with those already transparent. Thus to the initial animus of Mathilda corresponds the early animus of Léon (the assertive woman-child to the gun-toting assassin); in the second stage of their reflectivity, to the overt anima of Mathilda (as mother-nurturer) corresponds the repressed anima of Léon (the child-man); and in the final stage, to her animus-anima corresponds his anima-animus. Besson continues in his description of these two protagonists: 'il vit mais il est mort. Elle devrait mourir mais elle survit. Elle lui amène la vie. En acceptant, il accepte sa mort. Mourir pour donner la vie. Géométrique et cellulaire.'[16]

Besson's structuralist equation and organic bio-materialistic determinism should not delude the spectator from the fact that we are dealing here with the age-old myths of narcissism and the death instinct – even though, as we shall suggest in the next section, there are other ways to read the reiterative presence of death in this film. Nor should we fail to recognise the essentially chivalric but misogynistic message inherent in the above statement that man lays down his life for woman who gave him life. However, that being said, in relation to constructing subjectivity and the representation of sexuality, Besson does make clear that Logos/intellect and Eros/instinct, animus and anima, male and female, can cohabit in one person – albeit dangerously and at a price because the social structures in which we live bear such a deep animosity to it. Viewed in this light, regression and pathology, or the irruption of it, have positive compensatory value because of what is achieved: a better balance within the psyche. But whether this compensates for the lack of the father and mother is another question, which is what the next section will address.

15 *Ibid.*, 'so far apart, so different and yet so alike and close. Desiring the same love.'
16 *Ibid.*, 'he lives but is dead. She should die but she survives. She brings him life. In accepting it, he accepts his death. To die to give life. Geometric and cellular.'

Regression and pathology

The family in Besson's films is clearly a structuring absence, one might even say a destructured absence since it is so repeatedly disavowed from film to film. Besson's narratives are also so repetitively counter-Oedipal (not one protagonist gets to fulfil the trajectory successfully) that the question becomes whether, rather than counter-, these narratives are essentially anti-Oedipal? To say they are counter-Oedipal is to suggest that these films reveal the family and masculinity as being in crisis; to say that they are anti-Oedipal is to suggest that these films question the necessity of Oedipus, the union of sexuality and the nuclear familial complex. I think I have argued sufficiently the case for the counter-Oedipal nature of Besson's narratives; but I have hinted all along that there is something potentially quite productive in the regressive and even pathological behaviour of his protagonists. And this brings us to a consideration of the possible traces of the anti-Oedipus in his film narratives.

The Oedipal narrative is about the proscription of regression and the imposition of heterosexuality at the expense of desire (for the mother and father) which must be repressed. The Oedipal triangle (mother-father-and-child) is a construction that guarantees the perpetuation of capital and, of course, the ideal of the family. The child must evolve as the guarantor of the reproduction of the family and the guarantor of the circulation of capital. And so it goes on. The point is that the child-become-adult cannot regress from adulthood to childhood. This constitutes a basic challenge to the economic value of the family as protector of capital, as does the failure or the unwillingness to reproduce. And yet, in all of Besson's films there is the repeated image of regression. Jacques' orgasm in *Le Grand Bleu* is visually represented as a hallucination of his immersion in the sea – drowning in or copulating with the sea ('la mer'). Far from wishing to reproduce, Jacques hallucinates his own death in this sequence, a death he will subsequently experience for real when he takes to the deep blue at the end of the film. His regression is doubly marked. He copulates with his desired (but absent) symbolic mother ('la mer') *and* finds unity in his return to the symbolic mother's body through death. Nikita defies patriarchal law, first by masquerading as male and then finally by abandoning patriarchy altogether (by choosing/having to disappear). She refuses the recycling of her body by patriarchy as a reproducer of death – that which man most fears. In so doing, she becomes the absence that patriarchy so fervently wishes on woman and yet cannot countenance. For, in Oedipal terms, if the structuring absence of woman were to disappear, what material proof would man have of his own subjectivity? Nikita's self-removal (albeit an ineluctable decision) threatens the whole construct upon which patriarchy is based: sexual difference. Léon blows up the phallus – very anarchic – nothing left to reproduce with. And so on, all potential Oedipal familial triangulations are removed. The Oedipus does not seem very safe in all of this.

Gilles Deleuze and Felix Guattari have written persuasively about the negative effects of Freud's account of the Oedipal complex and the dogmatic function of 'Oedipus restrained' (the fulfilling of the Oedipal trajectory), so I will only summarily sketch-in their argument and what, in their minds, an anti-Oedipus position might be. The first effect of the Oedipal complex is to pathologise desire, particularly for the male child. The second effect is to reduce it to a heterosexual imperative. The father, by making sexual desire (for the mother) a taboo and by threatening the male child who disobeys him with castration, obliges the child to repress desire (his first knowledge of desire that is). Sexual desire for the father is equally taboo. Thus the male child must also repress homosexual desire. Henceforth, sexual desire must be programmed outside of the existing family and placed upon another object (the female other) and reproduction must now take place within a newly, but re-created nuclear family complex. Reproduction – recycling the family – is necessary to the functioning of capital just as much as is production. The family is the reproducing machine just as the industrial machine in advanced capitalism is the production machine. Sexual desire then gets repressed and displaced on to a more 'suitable' object (the female other). This is Freud's account of the desiring economy. It is not difficult to perceive that this economy of desire traps the child into an eternal cycle of repetition and that by 'boxing the life of the child up within the Oedipal complex' familial relations become 'the universal mediation of childhood'.[17] If this is the case then it is clear also that the unconscious gets a false start in life since it is dictated to from the outside, by the father, and not referred to by the child from within. Freud's (apparently totalising and uncompromising) version of the desiring economy means two things (at least). One, that heterosexuality is 'compulsory' and, two, that sexual desire must be restrained/contained within the heterosexual imperative of reproduction within the concept of family. If it is not, then, it is something for which we must feel guilt.

It is not difficult to see how mainstream cinema sells this family romance: melodrama sells us the notion of the family as the responsible, morally correct community within which we all want to live – it sanctions the desiring economy and privatises capitalism within the family; the western suggests that, even if the hero has to move on, nonetheless the community he has visited and in which he has restored order is now a safe place for men and women to get together and get on with their rightful purpose in life – reproducing it. The thriller and the gangster movies, the *film noir* – all punish the transgressive hero/heroine who refuses to play ball with this ideal familial construct. Ignore the heterosexual imperative at your peril and die; defect from the family and suffer alienation and shame. Defy patriarchal law at the cost of your life. So where in all of this do we find the production of sexual pleasure? The answer is that we do not. We either repress desire and carry on as if nothing had happened, or we throw ourselves into a paranoid pursuit of the death instinct.

Deleuze and Guattari remark that, as Foucault has noted, 'the relationship between madness and the family' can be traced back to this development in psychology of the Oedipal complex which invests the family with so much power.[18] This is undoubtedly why Jung took exception to Freud's view that neurosis inevitably

17 Gilles Deleuze and Felix Guattari (1984) *Anti-Oedipus: Capitalism and Schizophrenia* (trans. Robert Hurley, Mark Seem and Helen Lane; preface by Michel Foucault), London, The Athlone Press, 48–49.

18 *Ibid.*, 50.

originates in early childhood and that the Oedipal complex is a central effect of this neurosis. It makes no room for self-regulation, no space for the impact of the present on the psyche, and of course keeps the family intact as the moralising moderator of its members' behaviour. 'Oedipus', Deleuze and Guattari inform us, 'presupposes a fantastic repression of desiring-machines.'[19]

And it is here, in their notion of desiring-machines, that we perceive the germs of the anti-Oedipus. Deleuze and Guattari do not deny that there is an Oedipus sexuality, or an Oedipal castration complex; but what they do deny is that the Oedipal is formed in the unconscious. The Oedipal unconscious is a false unconscious forged by psychoanalysis which functions to keep in place patriarchy as the embodiment of power and the principle of advanced capitalism. The Oedipus sanctions the greater value (or only value) of the masculine sex. The effect of the Oedipal framework, of the familial triangulation, is to make possible the assigning of sexuality to one of the sexes and to ascribe lack to the other.[20] To rephrase Judith Butler,[21] the trick is to make one body matter and the other not – that is, to draw the distinction between bodies that matter and those that do not, to initiate the long chain of binary oppositions that construct our social sexuality. The first advantage of talking in terms of desiring-machines in relation to human beings is of course that they are not gender-specified. It empties out the need for a discourse that revolves around the struggle for the phallus and the concomitant anthropomorphic representation of sex (as male).[22]

What are these desiring-machines and how do they work anti-Oedipally? Deleuze and Guattari argue that everything is a machine and is connected to the body, to the desiring-machine. The desiring-machine makes us an organism whose mode of presence resides in the multiplicity of its disparate elements. This means we are in effect desiring-machines in the plural. The desiring-machine is not therefore a unified subject, nor does it need or seek

19 *Ibid.*, 3.
20 *Ibid.*, 73.
21 See Judith Butler (1993) *Bodies that Matter*, London and New York, Routledge.
22 Deleuze and Guattari (1984) 323.

to be. Rather, it is a linear and a disparate set of machines, and it is always in movement. Thus an organ-machine (our body with organs) is connected to an energy-machine which is connected to a production-machine, and so on. All of these are disparate forms of desiring-machines. The mother's breast, for example, is a production-machine. When it feeds it is connected to the child's organ-machine which in turn constitutes one of the infant's desiring-machines. The mother, in this context, is of course also an organ-machine and desiring-machine since she desires to produce for her child. The fact of feeding the child is to connect it to an energy-machine (the mother's), the child's own organ-machine then, in turn, becomes an energy-machine, it is fuelled with energy, and it will go on to become a production-machine of its own (at its most basic through excreting). Desire, in this anti-Oedipal view, is not based on lack (the notion of sexual difference and the fear of castration), but in the idea of movement and the constant renewal and re-forming of that desire. Thus we can be several disparate desiring-machines both contiguously and simultaneously.

The notion of patriarchal law and our assimilation into it as our route to identity becomes, in this context, a meaningless one, and one that should be rejected say Deleuze and Guattari. The place of the unconscious should be evacuated of the Oedipus and left to represent itself as what it really is: partial objects 'in a state of dispersion such that one part is continually referring to a part from an entirely different machine'.[23] As part of that process of reference, the unconscious 'as a real subject has scattered an apparent residual and nomadic subject around the entire compass of its cycle'.[24] This subject is death. Death is felt in every feeling, every becoming. It is felt as emotion, delirium and hallucinations. It is within the unconscious but is constantly mediated between different parts of different machines, so is always already present within our conscious state. Death is part of life, we live towards it and then we finally die. We become death. Jean Cocteau once said that to film life was to film the process of death. It is a matter of

23 *Ibid.*, 323.
24 *Ibid.*, 330.

fact, not a matter of instinct. Thus, conclude Deleuze and Guattari, 'there is no death instinct because there is both the model and the experience of death in the unconscious'.[25] Death is neither an instinct nor a drive against the libido (the sexual drive) as Freud and his Oedipus would have it. Rather, it is part of the desiring-machine.[26] Viewed in this light, Jacques' choice of death in *Le Grand Bleu* becomes a logical expression of his desiring-machine. He had hallucinated this moment of death when he simultaneously experienced it as drowning (in his making love with Johana). But we recall also that he had earlier witnessed it as drowning in the form of his father's death. Léon's death is a desire to give over his organ-machine in order to give life (energy-machine) to Mathilda and the real chance to live the flow and movement of her many desiring-machines.

In all of this, Deleuze and Guattari are not arguing against the principle of the family but what they are arguing against is the construction of the family as an Oedipal triangle. 'It is not a question of denying the vital importance of parents or the love attachment of children to their mothers and fathers. It is a question of knowing what the place and the function of parents are within desiring-production, rather than doing the opposite and forcing the entire interplay of desiring-machines to fit the restricted code of Oedipus.'[27] The myth of Oedipus serves capitalism well (the family as privatised capital). But as with other signs of capitalism (consumer commodities) the Oedipus is closely associated with the abstract concept of death. How is this so? Within the Oedipal construct, sexuality is one and indivisible: it is heterosexual. Hence the need for the Oedipal triangulation to be closed up and governed by the embodiment of capitalism: the patriarch. In this process of naturalising sexuality as heterosexual sex, desire becomes equated with powerlessness. For, in the Oedipal triangle, who constructs, handles and agences desire? Who links desire with the fear of castration and death? The father. These equations can come only from the mouth of the patriarch,

25 *Ibid.*, 332.
26 *Ibid.*
27 *Ibid.*, 47.

the embodiment of power. His is the presence that disturbs the original axis of desire between child and mother. The Oedipal triangle denies any possibility that non-familial relations of desiring-production might exist. It sees the family as all. It is that principle which Deleuze and Guattari resist. It is also the equation of desire with powerlessness which they contest.

These avenues of thought give us another way of under-standing Besson's representation of the family, or rather lack of the family. The family lacks first and foremost because of the absence of the mother. Why the missing mother and why the presence – however fleeting – of 'fathers'? Why the motherless daughters in *Nikita* and *Léon* and why, conversely, the paternal parthenogenesis in *Nikita* (Bob re-creating Nikita) and paternal surrogacy in *Léon*, *Le Dernier Combat* and *Subway*? It is not difficult to see that the triangle is a powerful non-presence, that a singularly vital part of the triangulation has been lopped off (the mother). Misogyny is a part answer, but it is not enough, not least because of the strong representation of three major female protagonists in Besson's films: Héléna, Nikita and Mathilda. The point is that the triangle does not exist for the most part in a Besson film. And the question is why? Within a reading that forefronts the concept of Oedipus and the desiring economy, Besson's narratives stand as a refusal to reproduce (either the family or capital). The one exception is *Le Grand Bleu*, but the father, Jacques, learns of his paternity only at the very moment that he has decided to kill himself. So the triangle's base remains broken just the same.

Let us first have a look at this lack of the family through the Oedipal optic. According to the Oedipal triangulation, the mother and father are at the base of the triangle and the child at the vertex. To reproduce is to create a new triangle. The vertex of the former triangle now becomes the new base and the progeniture of that base becomes the new vertex. If this pattern is not followed, the principle of pairing that regulates the social production of children falls apart; and the relapse produces new forms of incest and homosexuality. Because it is based in the assumption that the triangle (the family) is all, this is the 'either/or' that the Oedipus sets before our consciousness: you either reproduce or you remain frozen within the existing triangle, 'dying all alone, incestuous, homosexual, and a zombie'.[28] The very thought is enough to drive you mad! If, however, you break the triangle, smash its base – as to all intents and purposes Besson's films do – then you challenge this imposition of a unifocal direction (compulsory heterosexuality) and univocal sex (male sexuality as the one that signifies). You also challenge the strait-jacketing of sexuality as either normal and heterosexual or abnormal and homosexual. There has to be more to life than an 'either/or'. How does Besson achieve this challenge?

In Besson's films, the normal and pathological worlds are indistinct. Indeed, in some, the normal is non-existent. The devastated world of *Le Dernier Combat* is an obvious example of the latter which is why the struggle for power and the struggle for the phallus is so futile – it has no meaning, the concept of the patriarchal family is all but dead. The symbolism of the doctor/surrogate-patriarch handing on the daughter to the son-in-law is evacuated of meaning since the father and the daughter are killed and the son has to go on to kill the already dying (because there is no hope of survival) to get his female.

But what about when the two worlds are indistinct (the normal and the pathological)? Nikita's rehabilitation, for example, is merely the substitution of one set of pathologies for another. She moves out of her world into a world of presumed order and normality. Neat rooms, cleanliness, discipline, this is her new world. There is no attempt to understand her condition by a reconstruction of her pathological world, that is, the one she came from before she entered the one provided for her by the State. She just slides along into a new world of surveillance and judgement that is still about drugs and death. She is drugged into this new life out of her former drugged life; she is trained up to kill without asking any questions; there is no way out of this world for her any more than there was out of the previous one except through her own 'death'. These two worlds are close to each other in their madness.

This first reading allows us to see how Besson challenges the Oedipal imperative. But he goes further. Within a (second) reading

28 *Ibid.*, 71.

of Besson's narratives that forefronts the desiring-machines, the absence of the mother comes to signify a rupture in the linear connection of desiring-production. A key element to the connectivity of desiring-machines is absent, therefore a key part of life and death is also missing. The absence of the mother means that the child is incompletely fed. Thus its own desiring-machine will malfunction – lacking energy, it will also fail to produce. The motherless daughters either cry out for their mother (Nikita) or attempt to reproduce her (Mathilda). The absence of the mother endangers the motherless daughters. Nikita 'dies', she calls out for her lost mother as she is injected with a substance she assumes is lethal but which in point of fact makes her over to the State, to Bob-the-father. Mathilda, in each of her quests for milk (the mother's production- and energy-machine) returns to her 'home' only to encounter a life-threatening situation. The loss of the mother is experienced as death, one's own. And it produces a form of schizophrenia, a manifest denial of the present in favour either of a regression to the past (Nikita) or a projection into the future (Mathilda). In the case of regression, the 'schizophrenic' expresses a desire to return to a moment when she or he was not conscious of being a desiring-machine. In other words, this regression takes the form of a desire to reject the desiring-machine in favour of a body without organs. Nikita's regressive retreat into infantile behaviour can be read in this light. In the case of projection, the 'schizophrenic' invents the self into the future as an over-producing-machine. Thus, Mathilda goes in the other direction from Nikita in her desire to invest her body as 'more than'.

De-compensation and over-compensation are the two converse strategies these daughters use to survive the missing mother – this pathological refuge to childhood or over-investment in womanhood marks the daughters' unconscious recognition that their past (the missing link of the mother) is unrecuperable in the present. The irretrievability of the past marks the daughters as without history, their history. And this is a condition of schizophrenia – a form of madness that spells out exactly what the problem is in the social construction of the family and the over-evaluation of the patriarch (as the single site of power). Lois

McNay, in her study of Foucault, makes the point that the tendency of the mentally ill to retreat into infantilism is related to the way in which 'the relation between childhood and adulthood is constructed in contemporary culture. If infantile behaviour is a refuge for the patient, it is partly because childhood is violently separated from adulthood.'[29]

In other words, the social conditions of existence demand that the relationship between mother and child be severed. We have discussed earlier why this should be so for the male child. But the above reading of Nikita and Mathilda's motherlessness suggests that more than severance is in play, rather total erasure. So the question now becomes, what are the reasons for this violence to the mother–daughter relationship? And what does it tell us about the social construction of the family? Naomi Scheman, in her very useful essay 'Missing Mothers/Desiring Daughters', argues that the roots for this violence do not simply reside in the 'daughter's need to love someone else'.[30] And the question is of course, who says that this need is so, why is this lesson necessary? The roots, Scheman asserts, 'lie in the way in which patriarchy demands that she learn that lesson – as a submission to male power, first in the person of her father, and as a renunciation of her belief in her mother's power and her hope for her own'.[31] The point, concludes Scheman, is to teach the daughter her powerlessness and to bring her to identify with 'a male-defined world',[32] that is, to see the way of the world through the father's eyes and accept the workings of masculinist power.

What is instructive about the daughters' learning trajectories in Besson's films *Nikita* and *Léon* is that ultimately these lessons either fail or do not prevail. And the point needs to be made that it is doubtless here where female spectators (at least) gain pleasure from viewing this failure, even though, as we shall argue, the

29 Lois McNay (1994) *Foucault: A Critical Introduction*, Cambridge, Polity Press, 17–18.

30 Naomi Scheman (1995) 'Missing Mothers/Desiring Daughters: Framing the Sight of Women', in C. A. Freeland and T. E. Warterburg (eds), *Philosophy and Film*, New York and London, Routledge, 100.

31 *Ibid.*

32 *Ibid.*

scenario for Nikita is far less positive than for Mathilda. Nikita experiences great difficulty learning to become a woman. She does, however, succeed briefly – even to the point of adopting the male gaze (her mission in Venice). But, for all that Bob and Amande (the older woman who has already submitted to male power) teach her to accept the workings of masculinist power, Nikita finally revolts. In her last mission she is pushed to the brink of madness at the horror of this power which she must embrace. Since she cannot be a desiring/production-machine in her own right, but only as an extension of male State power, only as fathered by Bob, she elects to become fatherless. The hope that woman born of man will identify with him crumbles before Bob's very eyes. Nikita quits and adopts a position of absence. Absence becomes a form of resistance: no one can teach or reach her now. Her power is to become the unembodied body without power. Paradoxically, there is considerable power in Nikita's disembodied powerlessness because she no longer functions as an assertion of male power – she marks through her absence: 'elle va nous manquer' ('*we* will miss her') declare Bob and Marco solemnly at the end of the film. By signifying as absence she throws back at them a reflection of a non-image, her own non-image, her very unrepresentability within the workings of masculinist power.

What of Mathilda? Her scenario is something of a utopia compared to Nikita's nightmare. Mathilda's mother is a non-presence, Mathilda at one point early in the film refers to her own self as absent, as dead (to the enquiring headmistress on the telephone). Death then is part of her life, part of her every becoming (as Deleuze and Guattari would put it). She seeks the good breast (the nurturing mother) and acts it to her baby brother. She then loses her family including the (bad-breasted) step-mother. All mothers then are done away with. She turns to the only person who can help her, Léon, who, for all his guns, comes to represent the non-phallic father. If anyone represents the phallic patriarch in her scenario it is Stansfield – the patriarch gone mad. In terms of teaching-lessons between the daughter and the father, the form is one of exchange. Mathilda provides Léon with certain visual skills: he learns to see (read and write). Léon provides her with other visual skills: she learns how to see the moving target and hit it. This is very different from the way Nikita is trained up to see with the male gaze. Mathilda's eyes are trained for her own purpose of production, to kill Stansfield (the predatory, dangerous patriarch). This suggests a linear exchange of skills, not a hierarchical one. And so we no longer need to read Mathilda's failure to fulfil her mission as a negative recouping back into a female position.

Nor do Mathilda and Léon occupy a single identificatory position. We see them in effect as desiring-machines in the plural. Thus, Mathilda can occupy numerous positions of desiring in relation to Léon (for nurture, energy, production and so on) even if not all can be satisfied by Léon's own set of desiring-machines. This allows us to take a positive reading of the sexual love she feels for Léon (which is explicitly set out in the longer version, shown only in France at present). Clearly the American producers took an Oedipal reading of the declaration of love that was cut. The closing shot, of Mathilda planting Léon's green plant out in the school grounds, acts metonymically for her multiple desiring. It is an act of love that extends across all desiring planes. Desire here represents itself as a movement, a flow of energy and production. The organ-machine (Mathilda as much as the plant) is given the food for renewal and fuel for growth. The maternal Mathilda and the lover Mathilda co-join with the daughter Mathilda in that moment of becoming and ending. Léon is dead but his plant and Mathilda, desiring-machines fed by his energy-machines, live on.

With *Nikita*, Besson reveals through the characterisation of his female protagonist the effects of suppressing desiring-machines. Regression-as-pathology in the final analysis serves as a powerful resister to that suppression if only because it serves to deconstruct and thereby expose the processes of masculinist power and female disempowerment. With *Léon* and his two central protagonists, Besson goes several steps further. This time, he sets out a mapping of a different form of desire that is not based in guilt or death or the family economics of desire. Once again regression-as-pathology is at work here, in the form of Léon, but so too is its counter-manifestation, progression-as-pathology (in the form of

Mathilda). Both function in this film as systems that challenge the hegemonic principle of the transcendental subject (belief in the universal rational male) and the Oedipal triangle. And in so doing the film leaves the field of desire wide open, challenges the belief that madness is the 'other' of reason. The film proposes that if the social construction of relations of power as exemplified by the family is such that it makes us retreat into schizophrenia as a defence mechanism, then there may be within that regression the seeds of resistance that make power relations as they exist unsafe and unstable.

Resistance and power relations

The above considerations bring me to my last point about constructing subjectivity in the absence of the father and the mother. The question of resistance and power relations. And it might be helpful to begin with some considerations about dominant cinematic conventions that prevail, even today, in relation to the representation of women and desire. For in this we can begin to understand how Besson, whilst working within established codes and conventions, nonetheless can be read against the grain. In other words, even at this level, Besson can be read as countering these codes whilst at the same time ambiguously seeming to reproduce them.

Much of mainstream cinema, particularly Hollywood cinema and even more specifically the comedy and the melodrama, sells (in one commodified narrative form or another) the heterosexual imperative. It does not simply sell the idea of the family as a good idea, it also manages to package, within that good idea, a sublimated form of paternal parthenogenisis. It is not quite that reproduction takes place without the mother but more the case that the daughter is constructed as a fathered female (commonly known as 'daddy's girl'). We have already discussed Laura Mulvey's concept of the gaze and the three positions of the camera in the previous chapter, so it will come as no great surprise when I say that the motivation behind the representation of the fathered female is one of control – control of the desiring gaze. How much easier this becomes if the mother is absent, or is represented as such (through her collusion with the father). Naomi Scheman in her essay suggests, quite rightly, that the motherlessness of the heroines is far from innocent when it occurs. Having evacuated the possibility of an all-female exchange of gazes, it is far easier for the male to frame the desiring female gaze. She gets to look at what he wants her to see. Women must look but they may not be the authors of what they see.[33] As soon as they look for themselves, as with Pandora's box, they are punished. Implicitly then, Scheman argues, only a fathered female can claim 'public empowerment or feminine sexual identity'.[34] She cannot attain public power or sexual identity *from* or *as* her mother's daughter.

When Nikita is reborn into the family of the State, it is clear that there is only one true parent, the father – as embodied by Bob. And we see Nikita being shaped, tamed and reformulated by him. She is institutionalised in all senses of the word. Her madness/ pathology is reduced to silence, her violence is tamed into a form of cheap labour, finally she is the object of scrutiny, constantly under the male gaze. When she looks and desires, as with Marco, it is clear that everything she does is observed. Bob even comes into Nikita's domestic sphere to make it absolutely crystal clear that she is unequivocally a fathered female and that she is his, Bob's, creation. We have said already that she gazes for the State, thus the fetishistic gaze that is imposed upon her by the male (Bob, the State) continues its unidirectional route through her eyes. Nikita does not return the gaze, but stays steadfastly stuck in it.

Fetishism in cinema does not simply serve to make the female safe as an object relation that is used by the male to disavow sexual difference. It is also part of the ideological operations at work in mainstream cinema to separate out female sexuality from motherhood. Mainstream cinema, particularly Hollywood, func- tions ideologically to separate the discourses of female sexuality and motherhood, precisely because patriarchy has difficulty com- bining the two (it cannot represent to itself the mother as a sexual

33 Naomi Scheman (1995) 104.
34 *Ibid.*, 94.

being). Thus the female is represented as nothing but her sexuality: as whore, vamp, etc.; or as everything but her sexuality: virgin, mother. She is either in excess or lack of sexuality. When she is in lack she is outside sexuality. When in excess, female sexuality is fetishised: 'that is all she is'. And in this respect, fetishism becomes a form of repressing motherhood – motherhood being that which, ineluctably, marks woman's difference from man. As woman, the message is clear: you cannot agence desire and be a mother, no more can you be publicly empowered (by having a job) and be a mother. If you attempt to agence desire, be a mother and be publicly empowered then you will be punished. We might like to believe that this is an arcane cinematic trope. Far from it: *Fatal Attraction*, Adrian Lyne, dates from 1987; *Thelma and Louise*, Ridley Scott, from 1991. The only time woman can combine female sexuality and public power is when it is sanctioned by the 'true' parent (the male).

What happens to the female in Besson's films? *Nikita* does not deviate from this construction of the female-as-fathered until the very end; Héléna in *Subway* is punished for having attempted to escape the all-pervasive eye of the father; Johana in *Le Grand Bleu* gets abandoned because it was her framing eye that brought Jacques to land to father her child. And a classical reading of *Léon* would suggest that even Mathilda gets punished for attempting to agence desire. What is different in Besson's films is that this retribution for agency is not confined to the female. Fred dies, Jacques dies, Léon dies. Why? Is it because the father is not there to sanction their desire? Is it because pathology is no longer the hidden repressed secret of men and the open fact of the hystericised female body? Why are Jacques and Léon's bodies so disciplined? Why is the body the focus and not the intellect? What has happened to the ideal of the transcendental male? Where is the inner disciplined man of reason? What I am proposing is that whilst a conventional reading of Besson's films makes it difficult to dismiss the fact that his representation of women is misogynistic, it is still possible to argue that, through the body of the male, he challenges the discourses surrounding subjectivity, sexuality and its construction. Besson shows us the male body as hystericised from within even though it is disciplined from without. By self-imploding, Léon becomes a desiring-machine without organs, the phallus is gone, blown away – hardly the behaviour of the transcendental disciplined rational male is it? By drowning, Jacques rejects the phallus (its function) and becomes, similarly, a desiring-machine without organs. The two men are just as fetishistically represented as any of the women: Jacques and his diving-suits, Léon and his gun-adorned body. Within the traditional codes of cinema, Fred, Jacques and Léon are feminised and are for the most part singularly lacking in desire, that is, in agencing sexual desire. Fred is far more motivated about getting his band of singing men together, Jacques is clearly more at home with his friend Enzo, Léon does not even know who Marilyn Monroe and Madonna are, let alone how to agence a desiring gaze.

Some feminists might argue that Besson is doing no more than representing masculinity in crisis, which is just another way of privileging the male over the female – of giving greater value to masculinity in crisis than questions of female identity/subjectivity, of recentring masculine discourses. Compelling though this argument may be, and undoubtedly Besson's position in relation to women is ambiguous, I would like to suggest that a different reading is possible. And for two reasons at least. First, Besson never allows the case for patriarchy to rest. The father may well hand on the daughter to the son in *Le Dernier Combat* but it is an illusory passage of rights. Patriarchy is dead and doomed in the lifeless environment of this post-holocaust world. Besson exposes the practices of patriarchy in a relentless manner in *Nikita*, and *she* does make her escape. The father is dead from the very beginning of *Le Grand Bleu* and his death so traumatises the young Jacques that he seeks every means to avoid reproducing patriarchy. Second, in Besson's films the central male protagonist (or at least the three I mention above) stands outside of the concept of sexual difference. Whether, as we have done in this chapter, we analyse Fred, Jacques or Léon's characterisation through the more traditional route of film psychoanalytic theory and the Oedipal trajectory or through the more controversial anti-Oedipal one, these men ultimately occupy a non-Oedipal position, which is in effect to stand outside the concept of difference. If difference falls away, then the chain of binary oppositions falls apart. It then follows that there is no need to deny homosocialism or homo-eroticism any more than there is a need to deny heterogeneity. This, then, is a first order of resistance to power relations. Let us now look at a second.

In the previous chapter I drew attention to the notion of history and postmodern society. I discussed how the more negative view of postmodernism sees it as lacking history and that one of the consequences of lacking history is to create a schizophrenic condition. The subject becomes fragmented in its attempt to represent its self to itself – how can it if it has no past to refer to? This lack of history may not, however, be all bad. And it is here that I would like to develop a second line of argument in relation to power relations and resistance in Besson's work. My argument is that the lack of nostalgia in Besson's films is a second order of resistance to dominant codes and conventions not only of main-stream cinema but of course of dominant ideology. This is to suggest that lack of nostalgia, such as it is represented in Besson's films, is not without its own ideological effect. Nostalgia, which has its roots in a sense of history, is a practice of valorising the past over the present and indeed the future. Nostalgia is a mental escape from the present but can take material form. We can re-create the past into the present – indeed we do this in cinema repeatedly through the heritage film. Lack of nostalgia can mean two things at least. First, it can represent a refusal to invest in the meaning of the past as having greater value than the present; and, second, it rejects the psychoanalytic notion that our present behavioural patterns are ruled by what was repressed into the unconscious in our childhood. Lack of nostalgia is a refusal of the over-confidence of the past as well as a rejection of the powerfully held view of the unconscious as terminally but hauntingly past-historic. Nostalgia is invoked as a criticism of the present. So a lack of nostalgia would suggest that we look critically to the past and not necessarily accept what has always already been there. This in turn would suggest that power relations come under scrutiny starting with the power relations of the past over the present.

Foucault talks about power being everywhere. Relationships of power, he argues, get repeated permanently and are entirely self-reproducing. Critics have suggested that if power is everywhere, then ultimately it is nowhere – which may in the final analysis be true (that is, that it is a fiction we imagine). However, Foucault's ideas around power relations are actually quite helpful because they give powerlessness a completely new meaning – one we have already discussed on several occasions throughout this book, that of powerlessness as resistance. If power is everywhere, then it follows that relations of power get mimicked all the way along the hierarchical chain of power. In his discussion of power relations, Foucault points to a multiplicity of positionings. Thus there are some positions where individuals have power, others where they do not. These positionings are also implicitly temporal as well as spatial (our positions of power shift over time and space). We are both a producer and a product of power.[35] And it is for this reason that Foucault argues that power comes from below. It is useful, he states, to see power as not hierarchicised from the top down but rather as being omnipresent since all social relations are power relations. Domination evolves from a complex set of power strategies or investments, which makes it possible to pinpoint not one source but, rather, several. Foucault also makes the point that, at all levels of power (stratifications), there are resistances to those power relations and that these resistances coexist alongside the nexus of power relations. That is, resistances are always present, they filter through social and institutional strata and leave their traces.[36] This means that they get caught up at some point within power relations (co-opted). But, no matter, since the resistances themselves (as a practice) have moved on. When he talks of power strategies and investment, Foucault means discourses which individuals are invested in over others; by resistance, he means discourses that contradict or counterpoint the workings of power relations and which, by resisting, expose the complex sets of

35 Michel Foucault (1977) *Discipline and Punish: The Birth of the Prison* (trans. A. Sheridan), New York, Pantheon, 194.
36 Michel Foucault (1978) *The History of Sexuality*, vol. I (trans. R. Hurley), New York, Pantheon, 93–96.

stratifications and power strategies.[37] Investments and resistances are always changing. And it is often the case that investments change as a result of resistances. A prime example of this evolution would be the bid for universal suffrage (whether it be in Europe, the United States or South Africa). Discourses of the existing political classes were invested in the then status quo, but resistances eventually pushed the boundaries. Thus, at first, universal suffrage meant white men of the propertied classes had the vote, then it extended to the white-male middle and working classes, later still it evolved to encompass white women, even later to men and women of colour. How it got there is through the many and varied resistances to the existing power relation.

Foucault stresses the importance of resistance to domination/dominant ideology rather than attempts to change it. To succeed in resistance, he argues, means only that one set of investments in power relations gets replaced by another set of investments that will, in turn, serve as a new form of domination. The important role of resistance is that it is always on-going and always exposing the systems of power relations. This means of course that someone or some group is always at the margins. Foucault somewhat idealistically insists that those of us who have been marginalised must continue to stay at the margins. Resistance resides in the power of the marginals to show their powerlessness.

Conclusion: power relations and Besson's films

If I have spent some time explaining this concept of power it is because it has some useful applications to Besson's work. I have already discussed individual representations of powerlessness as a system of power. I want now, by way of conclusion to this chapter, to discuss the representation of communities in Besson's films in relation to this question of power relations.

To be part of a community implies that we suppress ideas of difference, that we suppress heterogeneity, because of our supposed need to share common values. We are invested in discourses

37 *Ibid.*, 97.

that suppress heterogeneity. The idea of the community emanates from this belief that we do have ideas that we hold in common. Thus, we suppress or elect to suppress resistances to our community, including the voices of marginals. Communities hold together around the belief that they share a common identity that separates them off from the idea of the 'other'. They participate in what 'Derrida calls a metaphysics of presence and Adorno calls the logic of identity, a metaphysics that denies difference'.[38] This idea of unified identity means a community dissolves its differences to constitute a social wholeness. But of course this means a closed identity that is based on 'mutually exclusive oppositions'.[39] Power relations within the community invest in discourses that keep this social ideal safe. Thus, in this discourse, the community is the inside to the 'other' that is the outside. This is the metaphysics of presence which, because it is based in a primary set of oppositions (inside/outside), generates a further set of binary oppositions that are supposed to function as a stabilising effect for the community. Communities are construc-ted as social ideas where members are individuals but are fused to, rather than separated from, the social ideal. However, community also means the individual within that community is always being watched, is always the object of someone else's gaze to make sure the individual belongs (neighbourhood watch for example). It suggests that a community can count you in or count you out. You become disciplined as good or bad.

Communities in Besson's films give intriguing messages about power relations. In *Le Dernier Combat* the city as a community is dead. In *Subway*, the underground community, the city of marginalities, comes under threat, loses some of its members but looks set to carry on with its set of resistances to the hegemonic investment in capitalism. In *Le Grand Bleu*, the community dies as its heroes drop out of circulation after having tested the limits of body resistance to pressure. In *Nikita*, the

38 Iris Marion Young (1990) 'The Ideal Community and the Politics of Difference', in Linda Jackson (ed.), *Feminism/Postmodernism*, New York and London, Routledge, 304.

39 *Ibid.*, 303.

evidence is that the community of the policed State will continue its self-reproduction, exercising its power over the individual. So the only resistance in effect becomes the adoption of a permanent state of marginality (Foucault's ideal but not perhaps Nikita's). And, finally, in *Léon*, a corrupt community of police (an embodiment of institutional power) gets liquidated by a lone contract killer (an embodiment of underground power, and so a marginal). In this world-view, the marginals – those on the outside – for the most part get a 'better' deal, at least those who manage to stay alive on the margins do. Meanwhile, the forces of discipline and order, the police, the supposed staunch upholders and guardians of the social ideal, get very short shrift. Those on the outside gain a resistance victory of sorts. At the end of *Nikita*, the suggestion is that Nikita has marked two men of the inside (Bob and Marco: 'elle va nous manquer' – *we* will miss her) even as she has to maintain her position as outside. The system will go on, but at least her resistance has touched these two. Similarly, the conclusion of *Subway* intimates that those outside (Fred's rock-band in particular) have marked those inside (the concert-going audience of indisputable bourgeois respectability that claps along with the rock performance). At the end of *Léon*, Léon, single-bodiedly blows up an entire police outfit. He leaves an indelible trace on that community whose corrupt set of power relations he has helped to expose. Of course there is not much hope that his gesture has brought about radical change. He has, however, challenged the self-serving behaviour of an institutionalised and sanctioned system of discipline (the police) that considers itself immune to its own community's policing eye.

The death of the community in Besson's films, like the death of the family and the lack of desire to fulfil successfully the social order of things (the Oedipal trajectory in other words), represents three imbricated ways by which Besson's work challenges the notion of subjectivity as based in sexual difference and binary oppositions. It challenges the effect of patriarchy that is invested in this construction of subjectivity and which colonises the concept of sexuality as male and represents all else as 'other'. His work exposes male anxiety around female sexuality and patriarchy's strategy to make it safe through voyeurism and fetishism. One of the ways in which he achieves this is through the absence of the mother and the concomitant attempts of the patriarch to inscribe the female desiring gaze into paternal authority as a strategy of denying sexual difference. In his deaths of the community Besson shows how the social ideal that works to suppress differences is a reproduction on a wider scale of family power relations. He places power relations under scrutiny and reveals how they are based in a politics of inclusion and exclusion. However, his films give little suggestion that anything short of marginality is an answer to the permanent repetition of power relations. There is no hint, in Besson's films, that a politics of differences (based in differences) rather than oppositions is at all possible. In his bardic function (to return to a term Besson uses in relation to his work), the strongest message he delivers is ultimately one that denounces the politics of exclusion as it affects youth and gender. His films warn us that there is a price to pay for the inadvisable suppression of differences and the narrowed social ideal of a unified identity. Presently, however, those with power have, for the most part, failed to notice this.

Afterword

There is no single or simple line to pull or draw from the previous chapters. This book has attempted to give a broad overview of Besson's work to date and to provide an analysis of his films through a number of theoretical avenues in an attempt to show the many levels on which one can read the narratives. The visual excitement of a Besson movie must not be forgotten or lost in all of this. His films are brilliantly shot and edited. The music score is often loud and raucous, and it pulsates with energy.

Throughout the book, I have borne in mind the very great pleasure that my students derive from Besson's work and have tried to answer in my own mind why he has such popular appeal. Given that the world which he portrays for the spectator is so violent, uncaring and institutionally corrupt, it would be quite possible to find his films both repetitive and alienating. Such is not the case, however, as his huge audiences make clear. I have suggested that, whilst his narrative closure is often one of death, nonetheless the overriding message taken from his films is that there is hope. Hope comes in the form of creative choice for the protagonists even though it entails for nearly all a fatal ending. The point is, though, that each one chooses their end (even Nikita) and, as I have explained, that choice takes the form of a direct challenge and/or resistance to the major institutions that govern us – in particular the society of surveillance, the society of consumption, and the institutionally sanctioned notion of the family.

The other very significant appeal of Besson's work is of course visual pleasure. In its comic-ness and violence and, too, in its visual pyrotechnics, Besson's cinema is an exhibitionist cinema. In this regard, Besson's work is very much a reinvigoration of a long-standing tradition in popular cinema, one that goes back to the earliest days of cinema: that of the cinema of attractions.[1] Much as the early pioneers of cinema experimented with the new technology, so too is Besson a great experimenter. We recall his early fascination with the camera and the rigorousness with which he sticks to the scope camera so that he can produce the film effects he wants; we recall also that he does not cheat on his shots, they have to be achieved with the camera, not through the cutting and pasting of special effects. This using of the camera-apparatus as a 'magic wand', this perception of it as a box that produces illusion and that can be played with, is very much the tradition of the cinema of attractions and one that Besson reproduces in his own work. It is instructive that (as we mentioned in Chapter One) amongst the filmmakers Besson quotes as sources of inspiration he names Spielberg, Lucas and Coppola – all special effects roller-coaster moviemakers.[2] The roller-coaster narrative-visual line of Besson's own films recalls the precipitous nature of the early cinema chase sequences and spectacular acrobatics. The idea is to display what the camera can do and visually to engage the audience. In this early cinema of attractions there is little concern for narrative effect. Besson, as we know, claims that, until *Nikita*, his films privileged atmosphere over narrative. By his own admission, *Nikita* was his first film to tell a story. Be that as it may, the storyline in any Besson movie is never privileged over the effect – the visuals remain more strongly in our memory than the storyline. Similarly Besson's characters are, if not cyphers, not exactly strongly drawn characterisations. They lack depth, owe much to the *bande dessinée* tradition, and are as much a part of the

1 Tom Gunning has written the definitive essay on this cinema of attractions and I am drawing closely on his argument to make my points in this discussion of Besson's work. Tom Gunning 'The Cinema of Attractions: Early Film, Its Spectators and the Avant-Garde', *Wide-Angle*, vol. 8, no. 3/4, 1986.

2 For more detail on this cinema of effects, see *ibid.*

display, the cinema of attractions and effects, as is the actual work of the camera. Besson's cinema then is a cinema of spectacle.

The mystery that surrounds the making and the release of any of his films is also part of this spectacularisation effect. He engages, tantalises his audience to 'go and see'. How can he visually outdo, out-perform himself this time? That is our anticipatory question. Without doubt, Besson has brought the popular back into French cinema with an illustrious bang, just as he has brought audiences back into the cinema theatres. One goes to see and hear a Besson movie. We have awaited his *Cinquième Elément* with dread *and* anticipation. 'Roll-up, roll-up! *The Fifth Element* is next! Hold on to your seats ladies and gents, this is going to be a whopper!'

Postscript: The return to science fiction – *Le Cinquième Elément,* 1997

Luc Besson's *Le Cinquième Elément* appears in some respects to mark both a new departure in his work and the closure of a circle. Closure because in this film Besson returns to the generic form that launched his career, the science fiction. New departure or beginning of a new cycle because of the size of the undertaking (the budget of $90 million, cast size and the huge number of technical staff) and because the narrative has an explicit message of hope not found in his earlier films. Besson's concerns for his audience and his belief in his bardic function remain unchanged, however. As he says, his work is 'Mission Elastoplast', he can only hope to please his audience, he cannot reduce unemployment nor diminish social injustice, but he takes his mission very seriously.[1] And in this brief postscript I want to examine in what way this latest film of Besson's overlaps with the past work, moves away from it and at times even contradicts it.

The genesis of *Le Cinquième Elément* bears similarities with Besson's earlier film *Le Grand Bleu* in that he had written a rough sketch for it in his early, teen years. The story he wrote then (aged 15), entitled *Zaltman Bléros*, had been in his production plans since the mid-1980s – but it was the success of *Léon* that made it possible for him, finally, to obtain the huge budget from Gaumont to make the film ($90 million). Besson, in interviews, talks of having himself lived in this futuristic world of the twenty-third century and of having invented a life that people inhabited as

1 Interview in *Le Monde,* 9.5.97.

normal and everyday – a city life in a city-scape 200 storeys high into the sky and 200 storeys underground (the New York of *Léon* meets the Paris métro of *Subway*). What intrigued him was how people would lead their lives, how they would eat and sleep in such a world. And one of the amazing effects of his film is the naturalness and the comfortable way in which people inhabit this futuristic world (again parallels with the inhabitants of *Subway* spring to mind).

The film, shot in scope, is a virtuosity of vertical and horizontal lines – the very mechanics and interiority of film, according to Besson. The visuality of the film is deliberately non-illusionist, but 'in your face' and two-dimensional. A two-dimensionality we are already familar with in Besson's work especially since *Nikita*, when he teamed up with Thierry Arbogast as the cameraman. Arbogast shot *Le Cinquième Elément* and we recall his and Besson's predilection, with *Nikita* and *Léon*, for low-light shooting and the consequent effect on choice of shots – mostly medium and medium close-ups, which in scope aggressively brings the image into the face of the spectator, thus calling attention to the two-dimensionality of scope.

This flattening of the image which is the effect of scope is heightened, as always in a Besson film, by the strong influence of the *bande dessinée* (*BD*) on his work. Besson worked with eight cartoonists to achieve the effect he wanted, but most particularly he turned to one of France's best-known adult comic book artists, Jean Giraud, to design the décors for his futuristic film.[2] Giraud, whose work encompasses both the western and the sci-fi genres, is famous in France for his collaborative work with the late Jean-Michel Charlier with whom he produced the widely admired western series of *BD*s, *Lieutenant Blueberry*. Giraud also worked in the sci-fi genre, this time under the pseudonym Moebius, and amongst other comic books produced *Cinquième Essence* which he published under the parodically named press company Editions

2 Giraud is no stranger to film. His influence can be seen in *The Empire Strikes Back* (Irvin Kershner, 1980) and *Blade Runner* (Ridley Scott, 1982). He did the costumes for *Alien* (Ridley Scott, 1979), and the drawings for René Laloux's *Maîtres du Temps* (1982).

des Humanoïdes. Giraud's work is satirical, it parodies genre and sends up stereotypes. His sci-fi work is heavily inflected with surrealist fantasy and as such plays quite strongly with issues around sexuality – particularly the visible sexual markers of difference, male genitalia and female breasts. In Besson's film, this playfulness gets picked up in Jean-Paul Gaultier's costumes with the ice-cream cone-shaped breast designs of the steward-esses' dresses (in French blue) and the oversized cod-pieces on Zorg's evil thugs' bodies.

Luc Besson's *Le Cinquième Elément* opened the 50th Cannes Film Festival in May 1997. It met with the same critical disdain as *Le Grand Bleu* some nine years earlier. This time, however, even some of the popular film magazines dismissed Besson's latest film as leaving a lot to be desired. *Le Cinquième Elément* was criticised for being a film of pure effects, technique and technics and very little else. It is indeed a film of excess, a special effects blockbuster which some critics have accused of trying to imitate Hollywood and singularly failing, a poor pastiche of *Blade Runner* (Scott, 1982) – and so on. Shot in English, many French critics raised eyebrows at its opening the Cannes Film Festival, particularly on this its Golden Anniversary. How could the film's Frenchness be justified merely by the fact that it was French-produced? How could it be French given that it had been mostly made in the UK (Pinewood Studios), and that its visual effects – the computer-generated shots of twenty-third-century New York – were created in the USA (Digital Domain, California)?

To the criticisms that *Le Cinquième Elément* is poor-quality Hollywood, the answer has to be that it is not Hollywood at all. Indeed, as an interesting review in *Neon* makes clear, it violates all blockbuster rules.[3] There is no single big idea. It is ten movies all rolled into one – including *Metropolis* (Lang, 1926), *Blade Runner*, *Star Wars* (Lucas, 1977), *2001: A Space Odyssey* (Kubrick, 1968). As Besson said in an interview, no American major would have touched his script which in Hollywood would have cost $140m to produce. Nor would they have touched it because of Hollywood's

3 See Andrew Harrison's review article, 'New Adventures in Sci-fi', *Neon*, July 1997, 44–51.

golden rules for blockbusters: nothing foreign and nothing queer. And fancy allowing fashion to run amok with science fiction! *Le Cinquième Elément* is also not Hollywood because, although technology is foregrounded, so too are the multiple narrative lines and the diversity of characterisations (some might argue in the good Gallic tradition of the French farce).

As to its 'unfrenchness', first, Besson dislikes the idea that a film has to have a flag stuck on it, but adds that the creative staff were all French, and that of the 540 technicians working on the film, one-third were French, the rest were English. And of course the film is a French artefact in that it relies for its overall look on two French designers (Gaultier and Giraud) and as an export item will do much to acclaim fashion as a marker of French national identity.

Leaving aside the production criticisms, what of the film itself? Amongst the negative criticisms that could be levelled at this film it has to be said that *Le Cinquième Elément* is a film which runs dangerously close to being utterly 'politically incorrect' in that it could be read as homophobic, racist and sexist. So, once again, as with *Nikita* and *Léon*, we are faced with a difficult film to evaluate since visual pleasure may well be seen to be in conflict with the textual meanings, hidden and not so hidden. Interestingly, this film – much like *Diva* (Beineix, 1980), a film to which it makes a clear reference – does seem to suffer from a number of blind-nesses, particularly colour blindness. Blackness, it could be argued, is glossed over and neutralised or aestheticised. The leader of Zorg's thugs is a good example of this. He can switch his appear-ance and the colour of his skin and transform himself from monstrously ugly to beautifully black. If skin colour does not matter then why does the camera circle around him in medium close-up when he is in disguise as black? There are other problematic representations of blackness. The black president is an ineffectual puppet whose white military do not obey him.[4] And of course the 'outrageous' radio compère, the transvestite (or is she just a drag queen?) Ruby Rhod (embodied by Chris Tucker) would make any white liberal uncomfortable about questions of

4 Note that his name is President Lindberg, referring doubtless to the doomed aviator ace of the 1920s.

black representation. Compared to Ruby, Gary Oldman as Zorg embodies little more than a fey pastiche of queerdom. It is not clear whether Besson is playing with stereotypes and challenging our own assumptions around race and sexuality. Nor is it clear whether Ruby's eventual – but incidental – heroism is supposed to question representations of masculinity. As for Besson's representation of women, again this is problematic. So let us take this issue of sexuality and colour further.

To the extent that there is a sexual narrative to the film, then it is white heterosexuality that is foregrounded in *Le Cinquième Elément* in the form of the love story between Korben Dallas (Bruce Willis) and Leeloo (Milla Jovovich). But it is the colour of its fore-grounding that is so striking with the excessively white skin of Leeloo and the body of Dallas – the palpably physical action-man-hero whose white iconography (hair and eyes in particular) is set off by his dress-code and whose orange singlet links, matches him ineluctably to Leeloo (she of orange hair).[5] Even if there are momentary isolated flashes of flirtation between Ruby Rhod and Dallas, this whiff of homosexuality and mixed race sex is swiftly reclaimed into good straight (but still mixed race) sex with the numerous images of Ruby's seductions of the various and inter-changeable look-alike white stewardesses.[6] Ruby's sexual exploits do not convince nor are they particularly funny. Inside the camp man we disbelieve the lurking of a straight eroticism. In fact, rather than a sexual narrative it might be truer to say that *Le Cinquième Elément* is in many respects a camp film – camp which is of course all about sexual parody.[7] However, as such it marks less of an extreme departure from Besson's previous films than

5 Of course Bruce Willis is a walking intertext of white action-packed manhood. Even when miserably depleted, as in Terry Gwilliam's *Twelve Monkeys* (1990, and to which Besson's film gives more than a cursory nod), he still is the one who resolves the enigma and fights his way out of the oppressive regime and saves the world, etc.

6 It is not evident either that one of the stewardesses he 'seduces' is not in fact albino, which produces even more complex readings for us to bear in mind.

7 The whole launch of the film at Cannes could be seen as a form of 'hype-camp' with the cat-walk display of Gaultier's costumes prior to the screening of the film. And Besson clearly enjoyed all the flouncing and flap of the design world. In one interview he said: 'I like fashion people.' (*Empire*, no. 97, July 1997)

we might suspect. The homosocial and counter-Oedipal narratives of his earlier work find a natural if excessive outcome in this film that camps it up and laughs at masculinity for taking itself so seriously. And it is in its campness and excess that we can read this film as displaying resistance to the social order of things (which is one of the ways in which we read Besson's previous films). Excess in décor is matched by excess in clothes-design and in the sashaying performances of several male characters, most particularly Ruby Rhod who is an extraordinary hybrid of Ruby Wax and Prince – Ruby with a Rhod (undoubtedly). The effect of the world of fashion design brought into this film by the costumes of Jean-Paul Gaultier, the master of excess and camp, leaves its traces all over this film as indeed does the impact of the futuristic décor designed by Jean Giraud. Gaultier's high-camp meets Giraud's surreal masculinist décors. This melding of excesses may explain why the camp sits less uneasily than one might expect with the, by now, common reoccur-rence of misogyny in Besson's films. Or maybe it is because camp is such a 'male thing' that it takes its misogyny for granted.

Where any claim to resistance to the social order of things starts to break down in this film is in the misogynistic representation of Leeloo, the fifth element. In this context, her characterisation is consistent with that of her earlier sisters Nikita and Mathilda. A somewhat androgynous body (breasts strapped down for better measure), Leeloo, like Nikita before her, is reborn by man. Leeloo is literally rebuilt from the little that remains of her (a hand), thanks to the brilliance of man's bio-genetics/bio-clonology. Like Nikita and Mathilda she is the woman-child who needs a man to liberate her – which also means to educate her. She frequently adopts the foetal position (shades of Nikita) and yet she is supposedly the font of all knowledge, whose DNA structure puts ours to shame. Despite this, she arrives into this world speaking a language that no one but a monk (Cornelius, played by Ian Holm) understands and has to be re-educated from her seemingly primitive babble ('badaboom') into man's language and world-view of history which she learns by rote off the computer – more technology, more techno-babble/speak. The one tear she sheds at images of warfare (including images of the two holocausts of World War Two) reassures us that she is feminine and the agent of peace (the direct opposite of Nikita's tear – that of the killer-lover). Despite her incomprehension of man's brutality to man and mankind's drive to self-annihilation, and despite her own conviction to the contrary, Leeloo is in the end persuaded that man is worth saving after all and that love, as embodied by Korben Dallas, is a sufficient reason to want to save the world (which apparently only she can do as the fifth vital element). Importantly, however, she does not divulge the secrets of her magical powers to prevent world annihilation. The solution to the enigma (which she embodies in conjunction with the four more traditional elements) occurs thanks to the fast thinking and prescience of the male, Dallas who, like Prometheus before him, carries the fire (admittedly he has only one match left, but that is part of the suspense) and saves the day. It is in fact the male who resolves the enigma, the female who embodies it. The male-centred narrative prevails in this film just as it has done in all previous Besson films.

What marks this film of Besson's away from *Nikita* and *Léon* is of course the happy ending – although this happy ending is invisibilised, doubtless ironising Hollywood's own happy endings. It is invisibilised in that Leeloo and Dallas make love in a secreted if public sphere (we do not see them, we are only told they are there). And what makes this film a mirror in reverse to Besson's earlier sci-fi film *Le Dernier Combat* is that there is every conceivable hope that life will go on – albeit under the watchful eye of the bio-geneticists. Thus, the Oedipal trajectory does get fulfilled in *Le Cinquième Elément*, but not without some disconcerting (male wish-fulfilment) twists. This time, the male protagonist ends up with his 'female-other' (Leeloo) back in the self-same cocoon in which that 'female-other' was built back into life (as a super-organism). In other words, Dallas gets back into and makes love with Leeloo in the very 'womb' that re-created her. This is a sort of *Le Grand Bleu* with life, rather than death, in mind – an interesting but worrying shift from Jacques' earlier refusal to fulfill the trajectory by choosing death (with *la mer*). This time we are presented with a mythical trajectory that would allow the hero to get back to the womb with mother and the female other, and the whole encompassed within the controlling effect of male technology.

Besson meant this ending to be a happy ending. However, we know that his films have consistently shown a deep concern with the effects of technology and man's obsession with it. So this happy ending is redolent with paradoxes. As *Le Cinquième Elément* makes clear, we have moved three centuries along the line of technology but man's obsession with it has not abated, in fact it has got worse.[8] We are right in the middle of the world of male-centred genetic engineering: the 'womb' is male-made, Leeloo comes to life thanks to DNA technology and the brilliance of robotics (which literally stitches her up), and love is consumated within the male-made 'womb'. Full cycle for the male, therefore, from womb back to the womb with Dallas as a projection of every male fantasy. As with earlier films, however, this fantasy is double-edged, since the male and the female body are after all made over to the State.[9] Remember that at the very end of the film, the president (even if he is a somewhat ineffectual world leader) gives the two new lovers just twenty seconds to fulfill their inter-course – and he dismisses Dallas's mother from the end of a telephone. So the mother is still absent – at best a disembodied voice. And, once again, the patriarch either in the form of the president, or indeed the military leaders are the embodiments of State power. Reproduction is surveilled by them. They are, then, hardly distinct from the earlier embodiments of the State as seen in *Nikita*. They are merely more sympathetic because the film is intentionally light-hearted, not *noir* or dark (*Nikita* and *Le Dernier Combat* respectively). The happy ending – viewed in this light – should give cause for concern.

What of the female, Leeloo? Is she more than the sum of her two sisters (Nikita and Mathilda) before her? In terms of DNA she is the sum of their parts several times over. However, like Nikita, she is named (or has her name reshaped) by the first man she

8 And we note how the piles of waste, jetsam, are even greater and more alarming than in earlier films – particularly *Le Dernier Combat*.

9 Paranoia and fantasy are not necessarily that far removed from one another.

encounters – Dallas asks her to cut short the lengthy name he is first provided with (by Leeloo). Nikita, we recall, is renamed Marie by Bob, and her State code-name is Josephine. Leeloo is of course a diminutive name – hardly the appropriate name for a 'perfect being' because it brings her purported power down to size (as 'less than'). Like Nikita, but even better, she can out-kick any baddie (even if her kickstart comes from *Blade Runner*), and she is clearly very smart (at least at assimilating information). However, she becomes weak in knowledge and in power by the end of the film – ostensibly because she is so horrified at man's inhumanity to man – and is saved from death (as presumably is mankind) by the famous 'open sesame' of all hearts uttered by Dallas at the eleventh hour: 'I love you', he declares. It was clear from the very beginning of the film that the Oedipal trajectory was 'on' for Dallas (he was seeking the perfect woman) and that he succeeds in fulfilling it. It is less clear what Leeloo understands of all this. Her language is basic like that of a child (again echoes of Nikita); she strips off her clothes without thought – western thoughts about nudity that is! – unintentionally embarrassing her male entourage (two monks and Dallas, an ex-army officer).

Leeloo, as woman, rejects the effects of patriarchy (technologies of violence and war) and trivialises the male gaze. But there is no power of resistance in these positions, first, because even as she rejects patriarchal technology, she is nonetheless a product of it and, second, because although she 'rejects' the gaze (and Dallas's first intrusive kiss) she does not understand its meaning. She remains, therefore, quite a weak and meaningless characterisation and as such is a far lesser sum of the parts than her two predesisters. Conversely, Dallas is more assuredly male than earlier Besson heroes. To Leeloo's woman-child he is man-man. It takes his love of a woman to decide that he will 'conquer' the evil he has been willing to tolerate until now (in the form of Zorg and his oppressive regime). *Le Cinquième Elément* becomes then a chivalric space opera. Leeloo, for her part, is part and parcel of the womb and reproduction narrative. She is the necessary instrument/element to survival. Literally, without her the world would succumb to evil – would be wiped out. She knows where the lost stones are, with the Diva. But, we must recall that it is Dallas who discovers them hidden in the belly of the Diva who dies giving up the enwombed stones. So again the enigma is solved by the male. Leeloo is, then, a double-edged sign of survival and reproduction (rebirth is after all the necessary survival system of the human species). But she is ultimately controlled by man who can make and, therefore, unmake her. As such she is a very conventional female characterisation, fitting into (amongst others) the classic *film noir* genre of 'woman as enigma' and 'man as unravelling the enigma of woman'.

If we leave aside the effect of camp as resistance, it has to be said that the challenges that Besson's earlier films placed on the viability of the Oedipal trajectory and the fixity of masculine identity seem to have evaporated in this film and the narrative in this respect must be read as regressive. Even the attempts at the play with sexuality are less compellingly radical than in his previous work, and the representation of woman is even more disturbingly regressive than before. Thus, the new departure I spoke of at the beginning of this postscript does indeed remain at the level of the technological: the film is vertiginous in its horizontal and vertical speed and is a visual thrill. But for all that it moves forward apace in that regard, there are many backward glances to social structures of sex, gender and race that are far from liberating. I do not feel that the film can be read as a space opera that sends up stereotypes. Viewed in this context, the message of the film then is a conservative one and, in that respect at least, *Le Cinquième Elément* bears strong resemblance to a Hollywood product.

In the end 'good' triumphs over 'evil' in this oversized 'human-ated' scope cartoon. This most expensive French-produced film ever is also part of its excess-story. But the negative hype surround-ing the film in terms of its cost and its Hollywoodness tends to miss the point that in production terms Besson's film is (arguably) the biggest counter-Hollywood success story ever and that he and Gaumont have proved that Europe, indeed France, can be com-petitive with American action movies. Pre-sales world-wide and clever marketing strategies meant that Gaumont had recouped its outlay before shooting even began.[10] First-day release figures in France alone were a staggering 300 million spectators. And for all that one might criticise Besson for his extravagance, the fact remains that thanks to the profitability of his work, Gaumont can finance more risky ventures (such as a new Mathieu Kassovitz film, *Déjà vu*[11]) and, perhaps culminating irony of all, Jean-Luc Godard's *Histoire(s) du cinéma*.[12] The philosopher-guru of cinema (Godard) financed by the bard of grand spectacle (Besson) – who would have thought it possible?

10 See interview with the Head of Gaumont, Nicolas Seydoux in *Le Monde*, 8.5.97.

11 Mathieu Kassovitz has a small cameo part in *Le Cinquième Elément*.

12 It is also worth making the point that Besson recycles his successes by producing films himself through his own production companies (Films du Loup and Films du Dauphin), the latest of which was Gary Oldman's *Nil by Mouth*, 1997.

Index